Job Hunt Mastery

Unleashing the Power of Modern Tools and Networks for Career Triumph

Written by
Morgan E. Blake

Independently published

2024

Copyright © 2024 by Morgan E. Blake

All rights reserved.

No part of this publication may be reproduced, distributed, or transmitted in any form or by any means, including photocopying, recording, or other electronic or mechanical methods, without the prior written permission of the publisher, except in the case of brief quotations embodied in critical reviews and certain other noncommercial uses permitted by copyright law.

For permission requests, write to the publisher, addressed "Attention: Permissions Coordinator," at the address below.

info@socialized.cloud

Published by Morgan E. Blake

Book Layout ©2024 Morgan E. Blake

Cover Design ©2024 Morgan E. Blake

ISBN: 9798321802991

First Printing, 2024

Introduction: The Art of the Job Hunt in the Modern Era

Embracing the New Job Market Landscape

The landscape of the job market has undergone a **transformation** that is both exhilarating and daunting. As we stand at the precipice of this new era, it's imperative to recognize that the traditional pathways to employment have evolved, morphed by technological advancements, shifting economic tides, and a global workforce that is more interconnected than ever before. It's a realm where adaptability, digital literacy, and a proactive approach to networking are not just advantageous, but essential.

In delving into this new job market landscape, it's crucial to understand the forces at play. The digital revolution has not only changed the way we work but also how we **find work**. Online platforms, social media, and job boards have become the norm in job hunting, each with its own set of rules for engagement. The rise of remote work and the gig economy has further diversified the types of employment available, offering unprecedented flexibility but also new challenges in terms of job security and career progression.

But it's not just about the platforms; it's about the **people**. Networking has transcended the confines of industry conferences and business meetings. Today, it's about building meaningful connections online and offline, leveraging relationships to uncover opportunities that may never be advertised. The saying, "It's not what you know, but who you know," has never been more pertinent.

Moreover, the skills sought by employers are evolving. Beyond technical proficiency, there's a growing emphasis on soft skills such as critical thinking, emotional intelligence, and adaptability. The modern job seeker must be a chameleon, adept at showcasing not just their expertise but their ability to thrive in an ever-changing environment.

For those embarking on this journey, the approach must be multifaceted. It begins with a **self-assessment**—a deep dive into your skills, passions, and values to understand what you bring to the table and what you seek in your career. This foundation allows you to navigate the job market with purpose, targeting opportunities that align with your aspirations and values.

Equipped with this self-knowledge, the next step is to master the tools of the trade. From crafting a compelling online presence to optimizing your resume for applicant tracking systems, each action is a strategic step towards your goal. But remember, technology is a tool, not a panacea. The human element—your personal interactions, follow-ups, and the genuine interest you show in others—remains irreplaceable.

As we forge ahead, let us embrace this new job market landscape with **optimism** and **determination**. The challenges are real, but so are the opportunities. With the right strategies, a willingness to learn, and an open mind, the path to career success is within reach. This journey is about more than just finding a job; it's about carving out a fulfilling career in a world brimming with possibilities.

In the pages that follow, we will explore each of these facets in depth, equipping you with the knowledge, tools, and mindset to navigate the complexities of the modern job market. Together, we will chart a course towards **career triumph**, harnessing the power of modern tools and networks to achieve not just employment, but a role that resonates with your deepest professional aspirations and values.

The Philosophy Behind Effective Job Searching

At the heart of every successful job search lies a core philosophy, a guiding beacon that illuminates the path forward in the often tumultuous journey of finding one's place in the professional world. It's not merely about the mechanics of sending out resumes or mastering the art of interviews; it's about adopting a mindset that transforms challenges into opportunities, and uncertainties into stepping stones towards career fulfillment.

Understanding Yourself: The Keystone of Job Searching

The journey begins with a deep, introspective dive into who you are, what you value, and where your strengths lie. This self-awareness is crucial; it's the foundation upon which all other strategies are built. It's about aligning your career ambitions with your inner values and strengths, ensuring that your job search is not just a hunt for any job, but for the right job that resonates with your core being.

Adapting to Change: The Only Constant in the Job Market

In a world where industries evolve overnight and job roles transform at the blink of an eye, adaptability is not just an asset; it's a necessity. Embracing change, learning to ride the waves of industry shifts, and staying abreast of emerging trends are all part of a philosophy that views change not as a threat, but as an opportunity to grow, learn, and reinvent oneself.

The Power of Networking: Building Bridges, Not Just Contacts

Networking, in the context of effective job searching, goes beyond collecting business cards or adding connections on LinkedIn. It's about building genuine relationships, engaging in meaningful conversations, and offering value to others even before you seek their assistance. It's a philosophy that champions the idea of mutual growth and the power of community in propelling individuals towards their career goals.

Leveraging Technology: The Double-Edged Sword

In an age dominated by digital platforms, leveraging technology is indispensable in a job search. However, the philosophy here is to use technology not as a crutch but as a tool to amplify human capabilities. It's about finding a balance, where online applications, social media, and job portals serve to extend your reach, but not replace the personal touch and authenticity that come with direct interactions.

Resilience: The Art of Bouncing Back

The path to finding the right job is often fraught with rejections, missed opportunities, and setbacks. Adopting a resilient mindset, one that views failures as feedback, is key to maintaining momentum in your job search. It's about learning from each experience, refining your approach, and persisting with an unwavering belief in your capabilities.

A Lifelong Pursuit: Career Development as a Continuous Journey

Finally, effective job searching is underpinned by the philosophy that career development is a lifelong journey. It doesn't end with securing a job; it's an ongoing process of learning, growing, and evolving. It's about staying curious, seeking new challenges, and continuously setting higher benchmarks for personal and professional growth.

In embracing these philosophical tenets, job seekers are not just preparing themselves for the job market of today but are also laying the groundwork for a fulfilling career that can withstand the test of time and change. As we delve deeper into the practical aspects of job searching in the subsequent chapters, remember that it is this foundational philosophy that will guide your way, ensuring that your search is not just effective but also enriching and transformative.

By adopting a holistic and mindful approach, outlined in this philosophy, you're not merely searching for a job; you're crafting a career that's in harmony with your deepest aspirations and potential. This is the essence of true job hunt mastery, a blend of inner wisdom and outer strategies, leading you towards not just a job, but a calling.

Chapter 1: Laying the Groundwork for Success

Self-Assessment: Identifying Your Unique Skills and Interests

Embarking on the journey of self-assessment is akin to setting the coordinates for a voyage into uncharted waters. It's about charting a course that is uniquely yours, guided by the stars of your skills, interests, and passions. This foundational step is not just about introspection; it's about laying the groundwork for a job search that is not only successful but also deeply fulfilling.

The Mirror of Self-Reflection

The process begins with holding up a mirror to oneself, a mirror that reflects not just the surface but the depths of your professional persona. This entails asking probing questions: What activities energize you? Which tasks do you find yourself drawn to, losing track of time as you delve into them? The answers to these questions are like signposts, pointing towards your core interests and passions.

Decoding Skills and Strengths

In this reflection, it's essential to differentiate between skills and strengths. Skills are learned abilities, honed through experience and education. They are the tools in your arsenal. Strengths, however, are innate; they are your natural talents and inclinations. Recognizing the interplay between your skills and strengths is crucial. It's about understanding not just what you can do, but what you do exceptionally well.

The Inventory of Achievements

Taking stock of past achievements is a vital part of self-assessment. This isn't just about listing job titles or roles but digging deeper into the impact you made. What were the challenges you faced, and how did you overcome them? How did your unique approach contribute to your successes? Each achievement is a puzzle piece, fitting into the larger picture of your professional identity.

The Landscape of Interests

Interests, unlike skills, are not about capability but about what captivates you. They are the themes and subjects that ignite your curiosity and drive your desire to explore and learn. Mapping out your interests helps in identifying career paths and roles that resonate with your core, ensuring that your job search aligns with what truly matters to you.

The Alignment of Values

Equally important in this journey of self-assessment is the alignment of personal values with professional aspirations. Your values are the compass that guides your decisions and actions. They reflect what you stand for and believe in. Understanding your values helps in targeting organizations and roles that not only appreciate your skills and interests but also share your principles.

The Power of Feedback

While self-assessment is an introspective process, external feedback can provide invaluable insights. Seeking perspectives from colleagues, mentors, and friends can shed light on strengths and talents you may have overlooked. It's about seeing yourself through the eyes of those who have witnessed your growth and contributions.

Crafting Your Professional Narrative

The culmination of this self-assessment process is the crafting of your professional narrative. This narrative weaves together your skills, interests, achievements, and values into a coherent story. It's a story that not only showcases your unique professional identity but also guides your future career trajectory.

As we delve deeper into the strategies and tools for an effective job search in the coming chapters, remember that the compass guiding this journey is the deep understanding of yourself garnered through self-assessment. It's this self-knowledge that will ensure your job search is not just a pursuit of employment but a journey towards a career that is as fulfilling as it is successful.

The path ahead is paved with opportunities waiting to be discovered. Armed with a profound understanding of your unique skills and interests, you're not just searching for a job; you're seeking a role that echoes your true self, promising not just employment but a career that feels like a calling. This self-assessment is the first step towards that horizon, setting the stage for a job search that is both strategic and soulful, grounded in the authentic expression of who you are and what you bring to the world of work.

Understanding the Employment Ecosystem

Navigating the employment ecosystem is akin to exploring a vast, dynamic biosphere, teeming with diverse opportunities, challenges, and pathways. It's an intricate landscape where various elements—industries, job markets, trends, and technologies—intertwine, creating a complex web of possibilities. To thrive in this ecosystem, one must understand its nature, adapt to its evolving conditions, and recognize the symbiotic relationships that define it.

The Industry Terrain: A Tapestry of Opportunities

The employment landscape is dotted with a myriad of industries, each with its unique characteristics, growth patterns, and demand cycles. From the steadfast realms of healthcare and education to the innovative frontiers of tech and green energy, understanding the nuances of these industries is crucial. It involves not just recognizing the current pillars of economic stability but also identifying emerging sectors poised for growth. This awareness enables job seekers to align their aspirations and skills with industries that offer not just employment but a future.

The Job Market Climate: Navigating Trends and Shifts

The job market is perpetually in flux, influenced by economic conditions, technological advancements, and societal shifts. Factors such as globalization, automation, and the gig economy have transformed traditional employment paradigms, giving rise to new job roles while rendering others obsolete. Staying attuned to these trends is essential for job seekers to remain relevant and competitive. It's about anticipating the winds of change and setting sail in directions that promise fruitful endeavors.

Technological Currents: The Winds of Change

In the digital age, technology is the wind that propels the employment ecosystem forward. Its pervasive influence reshapes industries, revolutionizes job functions, and creates new career landscapes. From AI and machine learning to blockchain and virtual reality, understanding the impact of these technologies is paramount. It's not merely about acquiring technical skills but grasping how digital transformation affects the very fabric of the job market and how it can be harnessed to carve out new career trajectories.

The Networking Web: Fostering Connections and Synergies

At the heart of the employment ecosystem lies the intricate web of networking. It's a vital component, fostering connections that can lead to opportunities, mentorship, and collaborations. Networking is not a mere exchange of contacts; it's about building relationships, sharing knowledge, and contributing to the professional community. In this interconnected landscape, the strength of one's network can be a significant determinant of career advancement and success.

Skill Evolution: Adapting to the Habitat

As the employment ecosystem evolves, so too must the inhabitants within it. The skills that were once in high demand may now be on the decline, replaced by new competencies that align with contemporary needs. This continuous skill evolution is a hallmark of the modern job market. Embracing lifelong learning, upskilling, and reskilling are not just strategies but essential survival mechanisms in this ever-changing environment.

Cultural Diversity: The Ecosystem's Rich Biodiversity

The modern workplace is characterized by its cultural diversity, mirroring the complex biodiversity of a thriving ecosystem. Appreciating, understanding, and leveraging this diversity is key to fostering an inclusive, dynamic, and innovative work environment. It's about recognizing the value that diverse perspectives and backgrounds bring to problem-solving, creativity, and business strategy.

In navigating this vast employment ecosystem, the journey is both exhilarating and daunting. It requires a keen eye for opportunity, a willingness to adapt, and an unwavering commitment to personal and professional growth. As we delve deeper into the strategies and tools in the subsequent sections, remember that understanding the ecosystem is just the beginning. It's the application of this knowledge, combined with a proactive and adaptable approach, that will guide you through the intricacies of the job market, leading you towards a fulfilling and prosperous career path.

The voyage through the employment ecosystem is one of discovery, learning, and adaptation. Armed with a deep understanding of its dynamics, you're not merely a participant in the job market; you're a navigator, charting a course towards your own definition of career success. This chapter lays the foundation for that journey, offering insights and perspectives that illuminate the path ahead, guiding you through the vibrant landscape of modern employment towards the realization of your career aspirations.

Setting Realistic and Ambitious Career Goals

The art of setting career goals lies at the intersection of ambition and realism, a delicate balance that propels us forward while keeping our aspirations grounded in achievable realities. It's about envisioning a future that excites us, challenges us, and yet remains within the realm of possibility. This process is not merely about listing desires; it's a strategic planning exercise that requires introspection, market understanding, and a clear vision of what we seek to achieve in our professional lives.

Crafting a Vision: The Blueprint of Your Future Begin by envisioning where you want to be in the next five, ten, or even twenty years. This vision should not be confined to job titles or salary figures but should encompass the broader aspects of professional life, including the type of work, the impact you wish to make, and the values you want your career to reflect. It's about painting a vivid picture of your ideal professional future, one that resonates with your core beliefs and aspirations.

Breaking Down the Vision: Milestones and Steps

Once you have a clear vision, the next step is to break it down into tangible milestones. These milestones act as markers on your career path, offering a sense of direction and progress. For each milestone, identify specific, measurable, achievable, relevant, and time-bound (SMART) goals. For instance, if your vision includes leading a team, a milestone could be developing leadership skills, which can be broken down into goals like taking a leadership course or leading a project.

Market Alignment: Ensuring Your Goals Are In Sync With Reality

An essential aspect of setting realistic goals is aligning them with the current and future trends of the job market. This involves understanding the demand for certain skills, the growth trajectory of industries, and the impact of technological advancements. It's about ensuring that your goals are not just ambitious but also viable in the evolving employment landscape.

Flexibility: The Ability to Pivot

While it's crucial to have a clear set of goals, it's equally important to remain flexible. The job market is dynamic, and unforeseen opportunities and challenges can arise. Be prepared to reassess and adjust your goals as you gain new experiences, acquire new skills, and as the market conditions change. This adaptability ensures that your career goals remain relevant and achievable, even as the landscape shifts.

Action Plan: Mapping the Journey

With your goals set and aligned with the market, the next step is to create an action plan. This plan outlines the specific steps you need to take to achieve each goal. It could involve pursuing additional education, gaining particular experience, or building a network in your field of interest. Each action should be tied to a timeline, creating a roadmap that guides your career journey.

Accountability and Review: Keeping on Track

Setting goals is just the beginning; staying on course is where the challenge lies. Establish a system of accountability, whether it's through regular self-reviews, mentorship, or peer support. Regularly review your goals and progress, celebrating achievements and identifying areas that need adjustment. This ongoing process ensures that your career trajectory remains aligned with your evolving aspirations and the changing job market.

Integrating Personal and Professional Goals: A Holistic Approach

Finally, while setting career goals, it's important to consider how they fit within your broader life goals. Your career is a significant part of your life, but it's just one piece of the puzzle. Ensure that your professional aspirations complement your personal life, allowing for a balanced and fulfilling life journey.

In conclusion, setting realistic and ambitious career goals is a dynamic and continuous process that lies at the heart of career development. It's about knowing where you want to go, understanding the steps to get there, and being prepared to adapt as circumstances change. As we move forward in this book, keep in mind that these goals are not just destinations but beacons guiding your journey through the ever-evolving landscape of the job market. With a clear vision, a strategic plan, and a flexible approach, you're well-equipped to navigate the path to career success, turning aspirations into achievements.

Chapter 2: The Digital Toolbox: Online Resources and Platforms

Navigating Job Boards and Career Websites

In the digital age, job boards and career websites serve as the nerve centers of the job search process, a vast digital landscape brimming with opportunities. Yet, for many, this landscape can seem overwhelming, a labyrinth of options where opportunities can be both abundant and elusive. The key to navigating this complex terrain lies in adopting a strategic approach, one that goes beyond mere browsing to a targeted, efficient, and effective job hunt.

Understanding the Terrain: Job Boards and Career Websites

The first step in mastering this domain is to understand the variety of platforms available. From large-scale job boards like Indeed and Monster to niche sites dedicated to specific industries or professions, each platform has its unique advantages and audience. It's crucial to recognize the differences between general job boards, industry-specific websites, and company career pages, as each serves a different purpose and audience.

Creating a Strategic Approach: Quality Over Quantity

One common pitfall in the job search process is the 'spray and pray' approach, where one applies to as many jobs as possible, hoping for a hit. This strategy is not only inefficient but can also be counterproductive. Instead, adopt a quality-over-quantity approach. Carefully select positions that align closely with your skills, experiences, and career goals. Tailor your application for each role, emphasizing how your background makes you an ideal fit for the position.

Leveraging Advanced Search Features: The Key to Precision

To refine your search, utilize the advanced search features available on most job boards and career websites. These tools allow you to filter opportunities by keywords, location, company, job type, and more, enabling you to hone in on roles that match your specific criteria. By setting up customized alerts, you can ensure that you're promptly informed of new postings that meet your defined parameters, keeping you one step ahead in the job hunt game.

Researching Employers: Going Beyond the Job Posting

An effective job search involves more than just finding openings; it's about understanding the companies behind the postings. Use job boards and career websites as a starting point for deeper research into potential employers. Explore company profiles, read reviews from current and former employees on sites like Glassdoor, and delve into recent news articles to gain insights into the company culture, financial health, and industry standing. This informed approach not only aids in tailoring your application but also ensures that the company aligns with your values and career aspirations.

Networking and Engagement: The Human Element

While job boards and career websites are powerful tools, they are most effective when complemented by networking. Use these platforms to identify key industry players, potential employers, and networking events. Engage with companies of interest on social media, join relevant online forums, and participate in webinars and virtual job fairs. This proactive engagement demonstrates your interest and initiative, often making you a more memorable candidate.

Tracking and Organization: Navigating with Precision

Effective navigation requires meticulous organization. Keep a detailed record of where and when you've applied, including notes on follow-up actions. Use spreadsheet software or job search management tools to track your applications, responses, interview dates, and follow-up tasks. This systematic approach ensures that no opportunity falls through the cracks and allows you to analyze and refine your job search strategy over time.

Continuous Learning and Adaptation: Evolving with the Landscape

Finally, the digital job search landscape is ever-evolving, with new platforms, tools, and technologies emerging regularly. Stay informed about the latest trends in job searching, from AI-powered job matching services to new networking platforms. Embrace continuous learning, be willing to adapt your strategies, and remain open to exploring new tools and technologies that can enhance your job search.

In conclusion, navigating job boards and career websites with skill and strategy transforms the daunting task of job hunting into a manageable and even rewarding journey. By understanding the digital terrain, adopting a targeted approach, leveraging technology, and engaging proactively, you can uncover opportunities that are not just numerous but meaningful. As we move forward, remember that these platforms are but one piece of the broader job search puzzle, tools that, when used wisely, can lead you to the career opportunities you seek. Let this be your guide as you traverse the dynamic world of digital job searching, armed with knowledge, strategy, and the readiness to seize the opportunities that lie ahead.

Leveraging LinkedIn: Beyond the Basics

In the digital age, LinkedIn has emerged not just as a platform for professional networking but as a cornerstone of any strategic job search. Going beyond the basics of LinkedIn involves harnessing its full potential to not just connect but to stand out, engage, and secure opportunities in the ever-competitive job market. It's about transforming your LinkedIn presence from passive to dynamic, making it a powerful asset in your career advancement toolkit.

Crafting a Compelling Profile: Your Digital Handshake

Your LinkedIn profile is often the first impression you make on potential employers, recruiters, and networking contacts. It should go beyond a mere resume to tell your professional story. Start with a **professional photo** that conveys approachability and professionalism. Your **headline** should not just state your current position but encapsulate your value proposition, incorporating key skills and your unique selling points.

The **summary section** is your chance to shine, to convey your professional narrative, aspirations, and the value you bring. Use a tone that's authentic to you, and don't shy away from showcasing your personality. This section should weave together your skills, experiences, and goals, making a compelling case for why you stand out in your field.

Showcasing Your Experience: More Than a Job Title

Each position listed in your experience section should tell a story of challenges met, skills applied, and value delivered. Use **action verbs** and **quantifiable achievements** to demonstrate your impact. Incorporating rich media such as presentations, videos, or project summaries can further bring your contributions to life.

Skills and Endorsements: A Testament to Your Abilities

The skills section is not just a list; it's a curated showcase of your professional competencies. Prioritize skills that are most relevant and in demand in your industry, and actively seek endorsements from colleagues and peers. These endorsements serve as social proof of your abilities, adding credibility to your profile.

Recommendations: The Power of Professional Testimonials

Recommendations are personal testimonials that highlight your work ethic, accomplishments, and professional demeanor. They provide a multidimensional view of your professional persona, adding depth and authenticity to your profile. Aim to gather recommendations that cover a range of roles, projects, and skills, showcasing the breadth of your professional relationships and achievements.

Engaging with Content: Demonstrating Thought Leadership

Active engagement on LinkedIn goes beyond updating your profile. Share and comment on relevant industry news, write articles or posts that reflect your professional insights, and contribute to discussions. This engagement demonstrates your passion for your field, your knowledge, and your ability to communicate effectively. It's about positioning yourself as a thought leader and active participant in your professional community.

Networking Strategically: Building Meaningful Connections

LinkedIn is a powerful networking tool, but its value is maximized through strategic, meaningful connections. Connect with individuals in your industry, alumni from your alma mater, and professionals you admire. Personalize your connection requests with a note that explains the reason for reaching out, making it more likely they'll accept your invitation to connect. Remember, networking is a two-way street; look for ways to provide value to your connections, fostering genuine professional relationships.

Utilizing LinkedIn Jobs and Alerts: Staying Ahead of Opportunities

The LinkedIn Jobs section is a rich resource for opportunities, but its true power lies in its customization features. Use filters to narrow down roles by industry, function, level, and location. Set up job alerts based on your preferences, ensuring you're immediately notified of relevant postings. This proactive approach ensures you're always aware of opportunities, even if you're not actively job searching.

In weaving together these advanced strategies, LinkedIn becomes more than a platform; it transforms into a dynamic tool that actively contributes to your career growth. As we delve into the nuances of personal branding and networking in the following chapters, remember that your LinkedIn strategy is a central piece of this puzzle. It's about crafting a presence that not only showcases your skills and experiences but also actively engages with the professional world, opening doors to opportunities and connections that propel your career forward.

In this landscape of digital connectivity, mastering LinkedIn is akin to mastering the art of online professional branding and networking. With each interaction, post, and connection, you're building a digital footprint that reflects your professional journey, aspirations, and the unique value you bring to the table. Let your LinkedIn presence be a beacon, drawing in opportunities, connections, and ultimately, the career advancements you seek.

Utilizing Niche Industry Websites for Targeted Searches

In the vast expanse of the digital job search realm, niche industry websites emerge as beacons of targeted opportunity, guiding professionals toward specialized roles that align perfectly with their skills and passions. Unlike their broader counterparts, these platforms offer a curated experience, delving deep into the unique ecosystems of specific sectors. This focused approach not only refines the job search process but also unveils opportunities that might otherwise remain hidden in the more generalized arenas.

The Essence of Niche Job Boards: A Specialized Approach

Niche job boards cater to specific industries or professional communities, offering a tailored selection of opportunities that resonate with those deeply entrenched in or looking to enter particular fields. Whether it's healthcare, technology, arts, or non-profit work, these platforms aggregate listings that are relevant and appealing to professionals within these spheres, providing a more streamlined and efficient job search experience.

Identifying Relevant Niche Sites: The First Step to Targeted Search

The journey begins with identifying the right platforms that cater to your industry of interest. This requires research and due diligence, starting with professional associations, industry publications, and networking groups that often host job boards or recommend niche sites. Engaging with your professional network can also uncover valuable recommendations for industry-specific job boards that have proven useful to peers.

Creating a Standout Presence: Beyond the Basic Profile

On niche job boards, your profile should speak the language of your chosen industry, showcasing not only your skills and experiences but also your dedication and passion for the field. Use industry-specific terminology and highlight projects, achievements, and skills that are most valued in your sector. This tailored approach helps your profile resonate with recruiters and hiring managers who frequent these specialized platforms.

Leveraging Insights and Resources: More Than Job Listings

Niche websites often offer more than just job listings; they're a hub for valuable resources, insights, and trends within the industry. Engaging with this content can enhance your understanding of the sector's landscape, challenges, and opportunities. Participate in forums, read insightful articles, and attend webinars or online events hosted on the platform to deepen your industry knowledge and visibility.

Networking Within Niche Communities: Building Meaningful Connections

These specialized platforms are not just job hunting grounds; they are vibrant communities of like-minded professionals. Engage actively by joining discussions, connecting with other members, and sharing your insights or experiences. This active participation can elevate your profile within the community, opening doors to opportunities through direct recommendations or referrals.

Applying with Precision: Tailored Applications for Targeted Roles

When applying for roles found on niche job boards, tailor your application to reflect a deep understanding of the industry and the specific challenges and goals of the company. Highlight past experiences and projects that directly relate to the nuanced needs of the role you're applying for, demonstrating not only your suitability but also your enthusiasm for the specific field.

Staying Informed and Adaptable: Keeping Up with Industry Evolution

Industries evolve, and so do the job boards that serve them. Stay informed about new platforms, changes in existing ones, and shifts in the industry's job market by regularly reviewing and adjusting your job search strategy. Subscribe to newsletters, follow industry leaders on social media, and remain an active participant in the community to ensure you're always aligned with the latest trends and opportunities.

In conclusion, leveraging niche industry websites for your job search is akin to entering a well-curated gallery where every piece resonates with your professional soul. It's about immersing yourself in an environment where opportunities are not just abundant but relevant and meaningful. As we explore further into the nuances of effective job searching in the following sections, remember that these specialized platforms are a critical tool in your arsenal, one that can lead to opportunities that are not just jobs, but stepping stones in the fulfilling journey of your career. With a strategic approach, a deep understanding of your industry, and active engagement, these niche platforms can become gateways to your next great professional adventure.

Chapter 3: The Power of Networking: Strategies and Etiquette

Crafting Your Personal Brand

In the vast expanse of the professional world, your personal brand stands as your unique signature, a distinct blend of skills, experiences, and personal values that sets you apart. It's not merely about how you present yourself in resumes or interviews; it's the cohesive narrative that encompasses your professional persona across all platforms and interactions. Crafting a robust personal brand is akin to building a lighthouse that guides opportunities your way, illuminating your path in the crowded job market.

Defining Your Core: The Foundation of Your Brand

The journey of personal branding begins with introspection, a deep dive into the core of who you are as a professional. Identify your unique strengths, passions, and the values that drive you. Consider the aspects that consistently draw praise from colleagues or the projects where you've felt most engaged. These elements are the building blocks of your brand, the essence that will permeate every aspect of your professional presentation.

Articulating Your Value Proposition: Your Professional Promise

With a clear understanding of your core, the next step is to articulate your value proposition. This is a succinct statement that encapsulates what you bring to the table, how you solve problems, and the unique benefits of your approach. It's not just about the skills you possess but how those skills translate into tangible outcomes for employers or clients. Your value proposition should resonate through your LinkedIn headline, your networking conversations, and even the way you introduce yourself at professional gatherings.

Consistency Across Platforms: Unified and Cohesive

In today's digital age, your personal brand extends across various platforms, from LinkedIn to personal blogs, and even your email signature. Ensure consistency in how you present yourself across these mediums. This doesn't mean uniformity, but rather a cohesive thread that ties your presentations together, reinforcing your professional narrative. Whether it's the tone of your communications, the style of your resume, or the content you share on social media, each element should reflect and reinforce your brand.

Visibility and Thought Leadership: Sharing Your Insights

Building a personal brand also involves establishing yourself as a thought leader in your field. Share your insights, experiences, and perspectives through articles, blog posts, or LinkedIn updates. Engaging in relevant professional groups and discussions not only enhances your visibility but also demonstrates your engagement and expertise in your field. This active participation showcases your commitment to your profession and contributes to the community, further solidifying your brand.

Networking with Authenticity: Building Professional Relationships

Your personal brand is not just what you say about yourself; it's also reflected in how you interact with others. Approach networking with authenticity, seeking genuine connections rather than transactional contacts. Offer value and support to your network, whether through sharing information, providing introductions, or simply offering a listening ear. These genuine interactions foster trust and respect, key pillars of a strong personal brand.

Feedback and Evolution: A Dynamic Process

Your personal brand is not a static entity; it evolves with your career and as you gain new experiences and insights. Seek feedback from trusted colleagues and mentors to understand how others perceive your brand. Be open to constructive criticism and use it as a foundation for growth. Continuously refine your brand, ensuring it accurately reflects your current professional identity and aspirations.

Living Your Brand: Beyond Online Presence

Finally, remember that your personal brand is not just an online persona; it's how you live out your professional values and promises in the real world. From the quality of your work to your interactions with colleagues and clients, every touchpoint is an opportunity to reinforce your brand. Your brand should be a true reflection of your professional self, guiding your actions and decisions.

In conclusion, crafting your personal brand is a journey that requires introspection, consistency, and active engagement in your professional sphere. It's about defining what sets you apart, articulating your value, and living out that promise in every aspect of your professional life. As you progress through this book, consider how each strategy and tool can be leveraged to enhance your personal brand, turning it into a powerful beacon that attracts the right opportunities, networks, and career paths. Your personal brand is the narrative of your professional journey; make it a story worth telling.

Effective Networking: Online and Offline Tactics

In the intricate dance of career progression, effective networking emerges as a pivotal movement, a dynamic interplay between online engagement and offline encounters. It's the art of cultivating meaningful connections, not merely for the sake of adding contacts but for building relationships that are mutually enriching. This delicate balance between digital and physical networking realms requires a nuanced approach, blending traditional interpersonal skills with modern digital communication strategies.

Online Networking: Harnessing the Power of Digital Platforms

In the digital age, platforms like LinkedIn, Twitter, and industry-specific forums offer unprecedented opportunities to connect with professionals worldwide. However, effective online networking transcends mere connection requests or followers; it's about engaging in meaningful conversations, sharing insights, and contributing value to discussions.

- **LinkedIn**: Beyond connecting with peers, use LinkedIn to engage with content relevant to your industry, comment thoughtfully on posts, and share articles or insights that add value to your network. Join and participate in industry groups, not just as a passive member but as an active contributor.

- **Twitter and Other Social Media**: Follow industry leaders, join conversations using relevant hashtags, and share content that reflects your professional interests and expertise. The informal nature of platforms like Twitter allows for more casual interactions, but always maintain a professional tone.

- **Online Forums and Communities**: Identify online communities specific to your field. Engage in discussions, offer advice, and share experiences. These platforms often host a wealth of insider knowledge and can be excellent sources for learning and networking.

Offline Networking: The Irreplaceable Value of Personal Interaction

Despite the rise of digital platforms, the power of face-to-face networking remains unmatched. Conferences, seminars, and local meetups provide fertile ground for forging connections that often lead to opportunities, mentorships, and collaborations.

- **Industry Events**: Attend conferences, workshops, and seminars in your field. Prepare in advance by researching attendees and speakers you wish to connect with. Be ready with a succinct introduction of yourself that encapsulates your professional interests and goals.

- **Local Meetups and Professional Groups**: Join local chapters of professional organizations or meetups related to your industry. These smaller gatherings offer more intimate settings for networking, making it easier to engage in deeper conversations.

- **Informational Interviews**: Request informational interviews with professionals you admire. These one-on-one meetings are invaluable for gaining insights into your industry and building relationships with key individuals in your field.

Blending Online and Offline Tactics: A Synergistic Approach

The most effective networking strategy leverages both online and offline tactics, allowing each to complement and enhance the other.

- **From Online Connection to Offline Meeting**: Use online platforms to initiate connections but aim to transition significant interactions to face-to-face meetings, whether it's a coffee chat or a professional meetup.

- **Leveraging Offline Encounters for Online Engagement**: After meeting someone offline, follow up with a connection request on LinkedIn or another suitable platform. Share a personalized note referencing your meeting to reinforce the connection.

Networking Etiquette: The Art of Authentic Engagement

Whether online or offline, the cornerstone of effective networking is authenticity. Approach each interaction with genuine interest in the other person, focusing on how you can contribute to the relationship rather than what you can gain. Be generous with your knowledge, connections, and time, understanding that networking is a reciprocal process.

Follow-Up: Cultivating and Maintaining Connections

Networking doesn't end with the initial interaction. Follow up with new connections, expressing appreciation for their time and reiterating your interest in staying in touch. Share articles, events, or insights that you believe will be of interest to them, and check in periodically to maintain the relationship.

In conclusion, mastering the art of networking, both online and offline, is akin to weaving a rich tapestry of connections that can support, guide, and advance your career. It's about engaging with intention, contributing with generosity, and connecting with authenticity. As you journey through the labyrinth of career development, remember that each connection, each interaction, is a thread in the larger fabric of your professional network. Approach networking with strategic thoughtfulness, and watch as the tapestry of your career unfolds, vibrant and interconnected, leading you to paths untold and successes unimagined.

Informational Interviews: How to Approach and Benefit from Them

In the realm of strategic job hunting, informational interviews stand out as a profoundly effective tool, often overlooked in traditional job search strategies. These meetings are not about securing a job offer on the spot but rather about building relationships, gaining industry insights, and understanding the nuanced dynamics of your field from those who are actively navigating it. Approaching these conversations with the right mindset and preparation can unlock a wealth of knowledge and connections, setting a solid foundation for your career advancement.

The Essence of Informational Interviews: A Strategic Exploration

At their core, informational interviews are conversations where the goal is to seek advice and learn from someone's experience and perspective, not to ask for a job. They provide a unique opportunity to gain insider knowledge about the industry, company culture, and potential career paths that might not be evident from the outside. This exploration goes beyond surface-level interactions, delving into the depths of real-world professional experiences and insights.

Identifying Potential Interviewees: Casting a Wide Net

The first step in leveraging informational interviews is identifying individuals who can offer valuable insights into your areas of interest. Look beyond your immediate network to industry leaders, alumni from your alma mater, and professionals in roles or companies you admire. Utilize platforms like LinkedIn to research and connect, always personalizing your approach with a clear explanation of why you're seeking their insights.

Crafting Your Approach: The Art of the Ask

When reaching out for an informational interview, your request should be concise, respectful, and transparent. Explain how you came across their profile, why you're reaching out to them specifically, and what you hope to learn. Emphasize that you're seeking advice and insights, not a job, and propose a brief, convenient format for the conversation, such as a 15-20 minute phone call or coffee chat.

Preparation is Key: Doing Your Homework

Before the meeting, invest time in researching the person's career path, their current role, and the company they work for. Prepare thoughtful questions that reflect your genuine curiosity about their experiences and the industry. This preparation not only demonstrates your seriousness and respect for their time but also ensures you make the most of the opportunity to gather valuable insights.

Navigating the Conversation: Active Listening and Engagement

During the interview, your role is primarily that of an active listener and learner. Allow the conversation to flow naturally, but guide it with your prepared questions to ensure you cover key areas of interest. Express genuine curiosity and appreciation for their insights, and look for opportunities to delve deeper into topics that resonate with your career aspirations.

The Follow-Up: Cultivating a Lasting Connection

After the interview, a prompt and thoughtful thank you note is essential, expressing gratitude for their time and the insights shared. Mention specific advice or stories they provided that you found particularly valuable, reinforcing the personal connection. This follow-up is not the end but rather the beginning of a professional relationship that you should nurture over time, keeping them updated on your progress and continuing to engage with their work.

Leveraging Insights: Applying What You Learn

The real value of informational interviews lies in how you apply the insights gained. Use the knowledge to refine your career goals, tailor your job search strategy, and even enhance your resume and cover letters to better align with industry expectations. The perspectives shared can guide your professional development, helping you to focus your efforts in areas that are most beneficial for your career growth.

In conclusion, informational interviews are a critical component of a comprehensive job search and career development strategy. They offer a unique window into the realities of your chosen field, direct from those who are part of it. Approaching these conversations with respect, preparation, and genuine curiosity can open doors to not only valuable insights but also potential advocates and mentors in your professional journey. As you progress through your career, remember that each informational interview is not just a learning opportunity but a chance to expand your network and build lasting professional relationships that can support and enrich your career for years to come. This proactive approach to networking and learning epitomizes the essence of job hunt mastery, setting you on a path of continuous growth and opportunity.

Chapter 4: Crafting Winning Resumes and Cover Letters

The Art of Personalizing Your Application

In the competitive arena of job hunting, the art of personalizing your application is akin to crafting a key that perfectly fits the lock of your desired position. It's about going beyond the standard one-size-fits-all approach, tailoring your resume, cover letter, and even your digital presence to resonate with the specific role and company you're targeting. This personalized strategy not only showcases your relevant skills and experiences but also demonstrates your genuine interest and effort, setting you apart in a sea of applicants.

Understanding the Role and Company: The Foundation of Personalization

The cornerstone of personalization lies in your understanding of the role and the company. Dive deep into the job description, picking apart each requirement and responsibility to grasp the essence of what the employer is seeking. Research the company's culture, values, and recent achievements to get a sense of what they prioritize. This foundational knowledge will guide your customization efforts, ensuring that every element of your application speaks directly to their needs and ethos.

Customizing Your Resume: A Reflection of Fit and Value

Your resume should be a mirror reflecting the match between your skills and the job's requirements. Start by **highlighting experiences and skills** that align closely with the role, using the same language and terminology found in the job description. Incorporate **quantifiable achievements** that relate to the key outcomes the employer is seeking. For instance, if the role emphasizes leadership, detail specific instances where your leadership led to tangible results.

The Cover Letter: Your Narrative Bridge

The cover letter is where your application truly becomes personal. It's your opportunity to tell a story that connects your background directly to the role at hand. Use this space to explain why you're not just suitable for the role but passionate about it and how your values align with the company's mission. Mention any interactions you've had with the company or its employees and how those experiences reinforced your desire to apply. This narrative approach transforms your application from a mere submission into a compelling proposition.

Leveraging LinkedIn and Social Media: Consistent Personal Branding

Ensure your LinkedIn profile and other professional social media platforms complement your personalized application. Update your LinkedIn headline and summary to echo the core competencies and achievements you're highlighting in your application. Share content and engage in discussions relevant to the role and industry, demonstrating your active interest and expertise in the field.

Engagement and Follow-Up: Demonstrating Interest and Initiative

Personalization extends beyond the initial application. Engage with the company on social media, comment on their posts, and show your interest in their work. When following up on your application, reference specific points from your earlier interactions or your cover letter, reinforcing your keen interest and the alignment between your professional profile and the company's needs.

Seeking Feedback for Continuous Improvement

Each application is an opportunity to refine your approach. Seek feedback from mentors, peers, or even industry professionals on how to better personalize your applications. Use this feedback to continuously improve your customization tactics, making each application more targeted than the last.

In conclusion, personalizing your application is both an art and a strategic endeavor, requiring careful research, thoughtful reflection, and creative presentation. It's about crafting a narrative and a professional persona that resonates with the specific role and company, demonstrating not just your suitability but your unique value and passion. As we navigate further into the nuances of effective job searching, remember that personalization is your tool for making a memorable impression, one that can open doors to conversations, interviews, and ultimately, the opportunity you seek. Embrace this art, and let it guide you towards a successful career path, where each application you send out is a testament to your dedication and fit for the role.

Keywords and SEO: Optimizing for Applicant Tracking Systems

In the intricate dance of modern job hunting, understanding and optimizing for Applicant Tracking Systems (ATS) is akin to knowing the steps to a complex ballet—essential for a graceful performance in the job search arena. These systems, employed by a vast majority of companies, sift through countless applications to identify candidates who best match the job criteria. Mastery over ATS optimization not only ensures your application makes it through these digital gatekeepers but also highlights your adaptability to modern job search technologies.

Deciphering the Algorithm: Understanding ATS Mechanics

At its core, an ATS functions by scanning resumes and applications for specific keywords and phrases that match the job description. This process is not just about simple keyword matching but understanding the context and frequency of these terms within your application. It's crucial to grasp that these systems are designed to mirror the employer's priorities, filtering candidates based on how closely their resumes match the job specifications.

Strategic Keyword Integration: Speaking the ATS Language

The art of keyword optimization starts with a thorough analysis of the job description. Identify the skills, qualifications, and experiences that are repeatedly emphasized. These are your target keywords. Integrating these terms into your resume requires finesse—**they should flow naturally within your professional narrative, rather than being awkwardly stuffed**. Use these keywords to articulate your experiences, ensuring they're woven into descriptions of your responsibilities and achievements.

Beyond Keywords: The Nuance of SEO in Job Applications

Optimizing for ATS extends beyond mere keyword insertion. Consider the nuances of **Search Engine Optimization (SEO)**, where relevance and context play pivotal roles. Use industry-specific jargon and acronyms that a hiring manager would expect a qualified candidate to understand. Additionally, the placement of keywords matters—having them prominently featured in titles, headers, and the top third of your resume can increase their impact.

Formatting for Clarity: Making it ATS-Friendly

An ATS-friendly resume is also about smart formatting. Avoid overly complex layouts, graphics, and tables, as these can confuse the ATS. Stick to standard resume formats with clear headings for sections like Work Experience, Education, and Skills. Use bullet points to delineate job duties and achievements, ensuring each point contains relevant keywords and quantifiable outcomes when possible.

Customization is Key: Tailoring for Each Application

While it might be tempting to create a one-size-fits-all resume, customization is crucial in the ATS age. Tailor your resume for each application, emphasizing the keywords and qualifications that are most relevant to the specific role. This tailored approach not only helps in getting past the ATS but also demonstrates to potential employers that you've invested time and thought into your application, reflecting your genuine interest in the position.

Leveraging LinkedIn and Online Profiles for SEO

Your digital footprint, especially your LinkedIn profile, should echo the optimization of your resume. Ensure your LinkedIn headline, summary, and experience sections are rich with relevant keywords and industry terms. Engaging in professional groups, publishing relevant content, and maintaining an active presence can further enhance your visibility to both ATS and potential employers browsing LinkedIn for candidates.

Continuous Learning and Adaptation: Staying Ahead of the Curve

As ATS algorithms evolve, so should your understanding and strategies for optimization. Stay informed about the latest trends in resume writing and ATS technology. Experiment with different formats and keyword integrations, and seek feedback from career professionals or mentors who can provide insights into how effectively your resume communicates your fit for the role.

In conclusion, navigating the complexities of Applicant Tracking Systems is a critical skill in the modern job search repertoire. By understanding the mechanics of these systems, strategically integrating keywords, and maintaining ATS-friendly formatting, you position yourself to not just be seen by the ATS but to stand out. As we explore further into the intricacies of job hunting in the digital age, remember that your resume is more than a document—it's a tool, optimized and honed, ready to unlock the doors to your next career opportunity. Embrace the challenge of ATS optimization as a step towards mastering the art of modern job hunting, ensuring your journey towards career triumph is both strategic and successful.

Showcasing Achievements: Quantifying Success

In the landscape of job hunting, the ability to effectively showcase your achievements can set you apart from a sea of candidates. It's about translating your professional journey into a compelling narrative of success, where each achievement is not just stated but quantified, providing tangible evidence of your impact and value. This approach not only highlights your capabilities but also offers potential employers a clear vision of what you can bring to their organization.

The Power of Quantification: Making Success Measurable

Quantifying achievements means going beyond vague descriptors to present concrete, numerical evidence of your impact. It's the difference between stating "led a successful project" and "led a project that increased revenue by 20% within six months." This precision not only lends credibility to your claims but also helps hiring managers grasp the magnitude of your contributions.

Identifying Quantifiable Achievements: A Strategic Review

Begin by conducting a thorough review of your professional experiences, identifying instances where you directly contributed to positive outcomes. Look for achievements that can be measured in terms of growth, savings, efficiency improvements, or any other tangible metric. Consider sales targets exceeded, cost reductions achieved, timelines shortened, or satisfaction rates improved. These quantifiable outcomes form the backbone of your achievement showcase.

Crafting Achievement Statements: The Art of Precision and Relevance

Crafting achievement statements requires a balance between precision and relevance. Each statement should succinctly describe the action you took, the skills or knowledge you applied, and the quantifiable outcome. Use strong action verbs to start each statement, and ensure the achievements are aligned with the key requirements of the roles you're targeting. For instance, if the job emphasizes innovation, highlight achievements that demonstrate your creative problem-solving skills and the measurable impact of your innovations.

Contextualizing Achievements: Beyond Numbers

While numbers are compelling, they can be even more powerful when given context. Explain the challenges you faced and the strategies you employed to achieve those results. This contextualization not only adds depth to your achievements but also showcases your problem-solving abilities and resilience.

Incorporating Achievements Across Your Application Materials

Your resume should prominently feature your quantified achievements, particularly in the experience section under each relevant role. But don't stop there—your cover letter and LinkedIn profile are also prime real estate for highlighting your successes. In your cover letter, weave a narrative that links your achievements to the potential value you can bring to the prospective employer. On LinkedIn, use the projects and accomplishments sections to further detail your quantifiable successes, making your profile a rich testament to your capabilities.

Tailoring Achievements to Each Application: The Custom Fit

While you may have a broad range of achievements, it's crucial to tailor the ones you highlight to fit each specific application. Align your showcased achievements with the job description, emphasizing those that are most relevant to the role and company. This tailored approach not only demonstrates your suitability for the position but also your attentiveness to the employer's needs.

The Continuous Evolution of Your Achievement Portfolio

As your career progresses, so should your portfolio of achievements. Continuously update your resume, cover letter, and LinkedIn profile with new quantifiable successes. This practice not only keeps your application materials fresh but also encourages you to consistently strive for measurable impacts in your professional endeavors.

In conclusion, showcasing your achievements by quantifying success is an art form that requires thoughtful reflection, strategic selection, and precise articulation. It's about painting a vivid picture of your professional impact, one that resonates with clarity and persuasiveness. As we delve deeper into the strategies for career advancement, remember that your achievements are the milestones of your professional journey, each quantified success a beacon that guides potential employers to recognize the unique value you offer. Embrace this approach, and let your achievements speak volumes, paving the way to new opportunities and career heights.

Chapter 5: Acing the Interview and Beyond

Preparing for Different Types of Interviews

In the dynamic world of job hunting, mastering the interview process is akin to perfecting your performance in a multifaceted play. Each type of interview—be it traditional, behavioral, group, or virtual—demands its own set of strategies and preparations. Understanding the nuances of these various formats and tailoring your approach accordingly can significantly enhance your ability to connect with potential employers and showcase your best self.

Traditional Interviews: The Art of Conversational Mastery

Traditional interviews remain the cornerstone of the job selection process. These one-on-one conversations require a balanced preparation focusing on both the content and the delivery of your responses. Research the company extensively, understanding its values, culture, and recent developments. Prepare answers to common questions, but go beyond rehearsed responses to engage in a genuine dialogue. Practice articulating your experiences and skills in a way that aligns with the company's needs, weaving in quantifiable achievements to underscore your suitability for the role.

Behavioral Interviews: Storytelling with Purpose

Behavioral interviews delve into your past experiences, operating on the premise that past behavior is the best predictor of future performance. The key here is to prepare stories using the **STAR** method (Situation, Task, Action, Result), highlighting specific instances where you demonstrated the skills and qualities the employer seeks. Reflect on challenges you've faced, the strategies you employed to address them, and the outcomes of your actions. This approach not only showcases your problem-solving abilities but also your capacity to learn and grow from experiences.

Group Interviews: Navigating the Dynamics of Collective Evaluation

Group interviews, where multiple candidates are interviewed simultaneously, test your ability to interact within a team setting. Focus on displaying strong listening skills, respectful engagement with others, and clear, concise communication. Demonstrate leadership qualities without overshadowing fellow candidates, showing your ability to collaborate and elevate the group's performance. Balance assertiveness with empathy, ensuring your contributions are meaningful and reflective of your ability to work harmoniously in team environments.

Panel Interviews: Managing Multiple Evaluators

In panel interviews, facing several interviewers simultaneously can be daunting. Preparation involves not only understanding the company but also researching the panel members, if possible, to tailor your responses to their areas of expertise. During the interview, address each member with equal respect, making eye contact and directing responses to the individual who posed the question while being mindful of the broader audience. This format tests your ability to manage multiple relationships and communicate effectively in a complex social setting.

Virtual Interviews: Mastering the Digital Domain

The rise of remote work has popularized virtual interviews. Technical preparation is as crucial as content readiness—ensure a stable internet connection, a professional background, and familiarity with the video conferencing platform. Practice maintaining engagement through the camera, focusing on clear articulation and non-verbal cues like nodding and smiling to convey attentiveness. Virtual interviews demand a heightened awareness of how you present yourself digitally, emphasizing clarity, engagement, and professionalism.

Stress Interviews: Keeping Composure Under Pressure

While less common, stress interviews are designed to see how you handle pressure. Tactics might include challenging questions, interruptions, or long pauses. Preparation involves building resilience to unexpected scenarios, maintaining composure, and thinking on your feet. Practice stress management techniques and keep your responses focused and positive, demonstrating your ability to remain unflappable under challenging circumstances.

Preparation Beyond the Interview Type: The Holistic Approach

Regardless of the interview format, some strategies are universally beneficial. Develop a deep understanding of your own resume and the narrative you wish to convey. Practice mindfulness or stress-relief techniques to ensure you're mentally and emotionally present. Finally, prepare thoughtful questions to ask the interviewer, reflecting your interest in the role and your strategic thinking about how you can contribute to the company.

In conclusion, adeptly navigating the varied landscape of interviews requires a multifaceted preparation strategy, tailored to the specifics of each format. By understanding the unique challenges and opportunities each type of interview presents, you can craft an approach that showcases your skills, adaptability, and professional maturity. As we move forward in this journey of job hunt mastery, remember that each interview is an opportunity to learn and refine your approach, bringing you one step closer to your ideal career destination. Embrace the diversity of these experiences, and let them mold you into a versatile and compelling candidate, ready to thrive in the dynamic world of modern employment.

Communicating Your Value: Strategies for Success

In the intricate ballet of the job market, articulating your value is akin to performing a well-choreographed dance that captures the audience's attention. It's about more than listing skills and experiences; it's about weaving a compelling narrative that highlights your unique contributions, problem-solving abilities, and the tangible results you bring to the table. This chapter delves into the art of communicating your value, offering strategies that ensure your message resonates with clarity and impact, whether in your resume, during networking opportunities, or in the crucial moments of an interview.

Understanding Your Unique Selling Proposition (USP)

Your journey begins with identifying your USP—a blend of skills, experiences, and personal attributes that sets you apart. Reflect on your career highlights, projects you've spearheaded, challenges you've navigated, and the innovative solutions you've implemented. Consider feedback from peers and leaders, pinpointing the qualities they most frequently commend. Your USP is the cornerstone of your value narrative, encapsulating the essence of what you offer.

Crafting a Compelling Narrative

With your USP as the foundation, craft a narrative that showcases your journey, challenges you've overcome, and the quantifiable impact of your contributions. Employ storytelling techniques, framing your experiences within the **STAR** method (Situation, Task, Action, Result), to provide context and depth. This narrative should underscore not just what you've done, but how you've approached problems, collaborated with teams, and driven positive outcomes.

Elevating Your Resume and LinkedIn Profile

Your resume and LinkedIn profile are prime platforms for communicating your value. Each role listed should not merely describe duties but highlight achievements, quantified where possible, to demonstrate your impact. Use dynamic action verbs and industry-specific keywords to enhance visibility and resonance with ATS systems and hiring managers. Your LinkedIn profile, in addition to mirroring your resume's content, should also feature recommendations, endorsements, and contributions to discussions, further illustrating your expertise and engagement in your field.

Mastering the Elevator Pitch

Networking, whether online or in-person, requires a succinct yet powerful elevator pitch. This brief statement should encapsulate who you are, your key achievements, and your professional aspirations. Tailor your pitch to your audience, focusing on elements most relevant to the listener, and conclude with a question or statement that invites further conversation, transforming a brief interaction into a meaningful connection.

Interview Strategies: Demonstrating Value in Real-Time

In interviews, your ability to communicate value is put to the test. Anticipate questions related to your resume and prepare to discuss your experiences in detail, especially those that best illustrate your USP. Practice responses that highlight your problem-solving process, adaptability, and how you've achieved results, making your narrative both engaging and memorable. Use questions about challenges or failures as opportunities to showcase your resilience and capacity for growth.

Negotiating Offers: Articulating Your Worth

When the conversation turns to potential offers, your understanding of your value becomes crucial. Research industry standards for similar roles and consider your unique qualifications and the results you can deliver. Approach negotiations as a discussion about finding mutual value, emphasizing how your contributions will benefit the organization and justifying your compensation expectations based on the value you bring.

Continuous Self-Development and Reassessment

Communicating your value is an ongoing process, requiring continuous self-assessment and development. Stay abreast of industry trends, invest in learning new skills, and seek feedback to understand how your contributions are perceived. As your career evolves, so too should the narrative of your value, ensuring it remains relevant and compelling.

In conclusion, effectively communicating your value is a dynamic and multifaceted process, integral to every stage of your job search and career development. It's about confidently articulating not just what you've done, but how you've made a difference, showcasing the unique blend of skills and experiences that make you an invaluable asset. As we navigate the complexities of the job market together, remember that your value is not just in the roles you've held, but in the challenges you've overcome, the solutions you've crafted, and the positive impacts you've made. Embrace this narrative, and let it guide you to new opportunities and career successes.

Negotiating Offers and Evaluating Opportunities

The culmination of the job search journey often leads to the pivotal moment of negotiating offers and evaluating opportunities. This critical phase is not merely about agreeing to a salary; it's an intricate dance of aligning your career goals, values, and expectations with potential employers. It's here that your understanding of your worth and strategic foresight come into play, guiding you to make decisions that not only meet your immediate needs but also pave the way for future growth and fulfillment.

Understanding Your Worth: The Bedrock of Negotiation

Before entering any negotiation, it's imperative to have a clear understanding of your market value. This involves thorough research into industry standards, salary benchmarks, and the demand for your skill set. Tools like Glassdoor, PayScale, and LinkedIn Salary Insights offer valuable data, but don't overlook the insights from your network. Conversations with mentors, peers, and recruiters can provide real-world context to the numbers.

Comprehensive Evaluation: Beyond the Paycheck

When evaluating an offer, consider the total compensation package, including benefits, bonuses, stock options, and other perks. However, true job satisfaction extends beyond financial rewards. Reflect on the role's alignment with your career trajectory, the company culture, work-life balance, professional development opportunities, and the potential for future advancement. These elements collectively contribute to your long-term career satisfaction and growth.

Effective Negotiation Tactics: Balancing Assertiveness with Diplomacy

Negotiating an offer requires a delicate balance between assertiveness and diplomacy. Approach the conversation with a mindset of finding a mutually beneficial solution. Clearly communicate your value, referencing specific achievements and how they translate to potential contributions to the company. Be open about your expectations but also show flexibility, understanding that negotiation is a two-way process.

Leveraging Multiple Offers: A Strategic Advantage

If you find yourself with multiple job offers, use this to your advantage without compromising professionalism. Be transparent about your situation, as it can sometimes expedite the decision-making process or lead to improved offers. However, avoid using one offer merely as leverage against another in a way that could burn bridges.

The Art of Declining Gracefully: Maintaining Professional Relationships

Should you decide to decline an offer, do so with gratitude and professionalism. Express appreciation for the opportunity and provide a concise, respectful explanation for your decision. The goal is to maintain positive relationships, as the professional world is often smaller than it seems, and future paths may cross in unexpected ways.

Seeking Clarity and Confirmation: Ensuring Mutual Understanding

Once an agreement is reached, seek clarity on all aspects of the offer, requesting a written document that outlines the details. This ensures both parties have a mutual understanding and agreement on the terms, setting a clear foundation for your new professional endeavor.

Reflection and Forward-Thinking: The Path Ahead

Accepting a job offer is not the end of the road but the beginning of a new chapter in your career journey. Take a moment to reflect on the process, what you've learned about yourself, the market, and how you can apply these insights as you move forward in your role.

In conclusion, negotiating offers and evaluating opportunities is a critical juncture in the job search process, one that demands a thorough understanding of your value, strategic negotiation skills, and a holistic approach to decision-making. It's an opportunity to align your career path with your personal and professional goals, setting the stage for continued growth and satisfaction. As we navigate the ever-evolving job market, remember that each decision you make is a stepping stone in your career journey, leading you towards your ultimate vision of success. Embrace this process with confidence, knowing that you are equipped with the strategies and insights to make informed decisions that reflect your worth and aspirations.

Chapter 6: Navigating Job Market Challenges

Overcoming Common Obstacles in Job Searching

Navigating the job market can often feel like charting a course through uncharted waters, where unexpected obstacles can suddenly emerge, challenging your resolve and strategy. Overcoming these hurdles is not just about persistence but about adapting your tactics, honing your approach, and leveraging your experiences to turn potential setbacks into opportunities for growth. In this exploration, we'll delve into the most common obstacles encountered during the job search and outline effective strategies to surmount them, ensuring your journey towards career success remains steadfast.

Facing Rejection: Building Resilience and Insight

Rejection is an inevitable part of the job search process, yet each "no" carries valuable lessons. Instead of viewing rejections as setbacks, see them as feedback loops. Reflect on your applications and interviews to identify areas for improvement. If possible, seek constructive feedback from employers.

Use these insights to refine your approach, enhance your applications, and sharpen your interview skills. Remember, resilience is forged in the face of rejection, turning it into a stepping stone rather than a stumbling block.

Navigating the ATS Maze: Mastering the Digital Gatekeeper

Applicant Tracking Systems (ATS) can often feel like an impenetrable barrier, filtering out resumes before they reach human eyes. To overcome this obstacle, optimize your resume with relevant keywords and phrases that mirror the job description. Ensure your resume's format is ATS-friendly, using standard headings and avoiding complex designs or elements that could confuse the system. Regularly update your resume to reflect the latest trends and best practices in ATS optimization.

Bridging Employment Gaps: Crafting a Positive Narrative

Employment gaps, whether due to personal reasons, education, or involuntary unemployment, can be perceived as red flags by potential employers. Address these gaps proactively by focusing on how you've used the time productively. Whether through volunteering, freelancing, upskilling, or personal projects, highlight how these experiences have contributed to your professional growth. Frame your narrative positively, emphasizing resilience, adaptability, and the acquisition of new skills or insights.

Overcoming Overqualification Concerns: Balancing Expertise and Flexibility

Being perceived as overqualified can paradoxically become a barrier to securing a position. To navigate this, tailor your resume and cover letter to align more closely with the role's requirements, focusing on relevant skills and downplaying aspects that might overshadow the position. During interviews, address potential concerns directly, emphasizing your interest in the role, your commitment to contributing to the team, and your long-term career vision that aligns with the company's trajectory.

Expanding a Limited Network: Strategic Connection Building

A limited professional network can restrict your access to job opportunities and valuable industry insights. Expand your network by engaging in professional associations, online forums, and industry events. Leverage social media platforms, especially LinkedIn, to connect with industry professionals. Offer value in your interactions by sharing relevant content, participating in discussions, and offering your expertise. Remember, effective networking is about quality connections, not just quantity.

Staying Current in a Rapidly Evolving Job Market: Continuous Learning

The job market is in constant flux, with new skills, roles, and industries emerging regularly. Stay relevant by committing to continuous learning and professional development. Identify emerging trends within your industry and invest in acquiring new skills or certifications that align with these trends. Utilize online courses, workshops, and industry seminars to enhance your knowledge base and demonstrate your commitment to staying at the forefront of your field.

Maintaining Motivation: Setting Realistic Goals and Celebrating Progress

The job search can be a marathon, not a sprint, testing your motivation and endurance. Maintain momentum by setting realistic, achievable goals for your job search activities, such as the number of applications sent or networking events attended each week. Celebrate small victories and progress, whether it's securing an interview or expanding your network, to keep your spirits high and motivation intact.

In conclusion, overcoming the common obstacles in job searching is an integral part of the journey towards career success. It requires resilience, adaptability, continuous learning, and strategic networking. By addressing these challenges head-on with informed strategies and a positive mindset, you can navigate the complexities of the job market more effectively. Remember, each obstacle overcome not only brings you closer to your next opportunity but also strengthens your professional acumen, preparing you for the challenges and triumphs that lie ahead in your career path. Embrace these experiences as valuable lessons in your continuous journey of growth and success.

Embracing Career Transitions and Change

In the ever-evolving narrative of one's professional life, career transitions and changes stand as pivotal chapters, replete with both challenges and opportunities. These periods of transformation, whether prompted by personal choice or external circumstances, demand not just adaptation but an embracing of the new paths that unfold. Navigating these transitions successfully is about more than mere resilience; it's about leveraging change as a catalyst for growth, redefinition, and the pursuit of fulfilling career trajectories.

Understanding the Nature of Career Transitions

Career transitions can manifest in various forms: a leap into a new industry, a shift to a different role within the same field, or even the decision to pursue further education or entrepreneurial ventures. Each transition is unique, with its set of prerequisites, challenges, and learning curves. Acknowledging the specific nature of the transition you're facing is the first step in crafting a strategy that aligns with your goals and the new landscape you're entering.

Self-Assessment: Realigning Your Compass

As you stand at the crossroads of change, a thorough self-assessment becomes indispensable. Reflect on your skills, interests, values, and the aspects of work that bring you satisfaction and a sense of purpose. Tools such as SWOT analysis (Strengths, Weaknesses, Opportunities, Threats) can provide clarity, helping you to map out a career path that not only resonates with your professional identity but also aligns with the realities of the job market.

Skill Bridging: Building the Foundation for New Beginnings

Often, career transitions involve venturing into territories where your existing skills need to be complemented with new competencies. Identify the skills and knowledge essential for success in your new domain and pursue targeted learning opportunities. This could mean formal education, online courses, workshops, or even self-directed learning. The key is to create a bridge of skills that connects your past experiences with future aspirations.

Networking: Navigating the New Terrain with Allies

The role of networking cannot be overstated in the context of career transitions. Engage with professionals within your new chosen field, seeking insights, advice, and mentorship. Professional associations, networking events, and platforms like LinkedIn can be invaluable in this regard. Remember, networking is not just about finding opportunities; it's about building relationships and learning from the collective wisdom of your new professional community.

Personal Branding: Redefining Your Professional Identity

As you transition, your personal brand needs to evolve to reflect your new direction. Update your LinkedIn profile, resume, and other professional materials to highlight the skills and experiences that are most relevant to your new path. Craft a narrative that weaves your past experiences into a coherent story that supports your transition, demonstrating how your unique background is an asset in your new role or industry.

Embracing a Growth Mindset: The Learner's Journey

A growth mindset, characterized by the belief in one's ability to grow and adapt through effort and learning, is your greatest ally during transitions. Embrace the uncertainties and challenges as opportunities for growth, maintaining an attitude of curiosity and openness to learning. This mindset not only facilitates smoother transitions but also enriches your professional journey with continuous personal and professional development.

Practical Steps: From Planning to Action

With a clear understanding of your goals and the landscape ahead, devise a practical plan that outlines actionable steps for your transition. This plan should include skill development, networking strategies, personal branding efforts, and a timeline that guides your progress. Regularly review and adjust this plan as you gather insights and experiences along the way.

In conclusion, embracing career transitions and change is an integral part of the modern professional journey. It's about viewing each transition not as a disruption but as an opportunity to realign with your evolving career aspirations and to harness new possibilities for growth and fulfillment. As we delve further into the art of navigating the job market, remember that each transition is a chapter in your unique career story, filled with potential for development, discovery, and success. Embrace these changes with strategic planning, a learning mindset, and the courage to step into new territories, knowing that each step forward is a stride towards realizing your professional potential and aspirations.

Staying Motivated and Resilient

In the unfolding narrative of one's career, maintaining motivation and resilience amidst the ebb and flow of job searching is not merely beneficial—it's essential. These qualities act as the beacon that guides you through the fog of uncertainty, rejection, and the myriad challenges that the job market invariably presents. This journey demands not only a steadfast commitment to your goals but also the agility to navigate obstacles, learning from each experience to emerge stronger and more focused. Here, we delve into strategies and mindsets that underpin motivation and resilience, transforming the job search from a daunting endeavor into a journey of growth and self-discovery.

Cultivating a Growth Mindset: The Foundation of Resilience

At the heart of resilience lies a growth mindset—the belief that abilities and intelligence can be developed through dedication and hard work. This perspective encourages viewing challenges not as insurmountable barriers but as opportunities for learning and development. Embrace each phase of your job search as a chance to refine your skills, expand your knowledge, and build character. When faced with setbacks, ask yourself, "What can I learn from this?" This approach fosters resilience, turning potential discouragements into stepping stones towards your goals.

Setting Realistic, Achievable Goals: Navigating with Purpose

The journey of job searching is often marred by uncertainties and variables beyond your control. Setting clear, achievable goals can serve as your compass, providing direction and a sense of purpose. Break down your larger objectives into smaller, manageable tasks, such as tailoring your resume for specific roles, networking with a certain number of professionals weekly, or enhancing your skills in targeted areas. Celebrate each milestone, no matter how small, to acknowledge your progress and keep your spirits buoyed.

Maintaining a Balanced Perspective: Beyond the Job Search

While your career is a significant aspect of your life, it's crucial to maintain a balanced perspective, recognizing the value and fulfillment in other areas—be it family, hobbies, personal growth, or community involvement. Diversifying your sources of fulfillment can alleviate the pressure and disappointment that may come with job search challenges. Engage in activities that rejuvenate your spirit and provide a sense of accomplishment outside of your professional endeavors.

Leveraging Your Support System: Strength in Community

The path of job searching need not be a solitary one. Leverage your support system—friends, family, mentors, or career coaches—who can offer encouragement, provide constructive feedback, and share their own experiences. Surrounding yourself with a community that believes in your potential can significantly bolster your resilience and motivation, especially during moments of doubt or frustration.

Embracing Self-Care: The Reservoir of Strength

Self-care is paramount in maintaining motivation and resilience. It's the reservoir from which you draw strength, clarity, and focus. Prioritize activities that nurture your physical, mental, and emotional well-being, whether it's exercise, meditation, reading, or simply taking time to rest and recharge. Recognizing the signs of burnout and proactively addressing them through self-care can preserve your energy and optimism throughout your job search journey.

Adopting a Long-Term Vision: Navigating the Bigger Picture

While the immediate goal is to secure a job, adopting a long-term vision for your career can provide a broader perspective, making temporary setbacks less daunting. Visualize where you want to be in five, ten, or fifteen years, and understand that each step, even the challenging ones, is part of a larger journey toward that vision. This long-term perspective fosters resilience, enabling you to navigate the ups and downs of the job search with a sense of purpose and direction.

In conclusion, staying motivated and resilient in the face of job search challenges is a dynamic process that involves cultivating a growth mindset, setting achievable goals, maintaining a balanced perspective, leveraging your support system, embracing self-care, and adopting a long-term vision. These strategies not only equip you to navigate the complexities of the job market but also contribute to personal growth and professional development. As we journey through the multifaceted landscape of job hunting, remember that motivation and resilience are not just about enduring but about thriving, learning, and evolving. Embrace these qualities as your allies, and let them guide you toward not just a successful career but a fulfilling life journey.

Chapter 7: The Future of Job Hunting: Trends and Predictions

Emerging Technologies and Their Impact on Job Searching

In the grand tapestry of modern career navigation, the role of emerging technologies cannot be overstated. As we stand on the cusp of a new era, these innovations are not merely tools but catalysts that are reshaping the landscape of job searching, offering new avenues for connection, exploration, and engagement. The digital revolution has ushered in a paradigm shift, where Artificial Intelligence (AI), Machine Learning (ML), Big Data, and Virtual Reality (VR) are not just buzzwords but integral components of a job seeker's arsenal. This chapter delves deep into the profound impact of these technologies, unraveling how they redefine job searching in a digitally interconnected world.

Artificial Intelligence and Machine Learning: Personalizing the Job Search

AI and ML have transformed job boards and career websites from mere repositories of listings into dynamic platforms that offer personalized job recommendations. By analyzing your resume, past searches, and application history, these intelligent systems can match you with opportunities that align closely with your skills, experiences, and career aspirations. Furthermore, AI-powered chatbots provide real-time assistance, answering queries and guiding job seekers through the application process, making job searching more interactive and responsive.

Big Data: Insights and Opportunities

The proliferation of Big Data has provided unprecedented insights into job market trends, skill demand, and salary benchmarks. By harnessing this vast repository of information, job seekers can make data-driven decisions, tailoring their career paths to align with market realities. Big Data analytics also empower candidates to identify growth industries, emerging job roles, and the skills required to thrive in them, enabling a strategic approach to career development and job searching.

Virtual Reality: The Future of Recruitment and Onboarding

Virtual Reality is redefining the recruitment process, offering immersive experiences that allow candidates to explore company cultures, work environments, and even simulate job tasks from the comfort of their homes. This technology not only enhances the candidate's understanding of potential roles but also enables employers to assess a candidate's fit and skills in a more interactive and engaging manner. VR's potential extends to onboarding, providing new hires with a virtual introduction to their workplace, team, and roles, thus smoothing the transition into new positions.

Blockchain: Credential Verification and Trust

Blockchain technology is emerging as a powerful tool for credential verification, enabling job seekers to securely store and share verified educational qualifications and professional achievements. This immutable record reduces the risk of fraudulent claims, streamlining the hiring process and enhancing trust between candidates and employers. For job seekers, blockchain presents an opportunity to create a transparent, verifiable professional profile that stands out in a competitive job market.

Social Media and Networking Platforms: Expanding Horizons

While not new, the role of social media and professional networking platforms like LinkedIn continues to evolve, powered by advancements in technology. These platforms are becoming increasingly sophisticated, facilitating not just networking but also personal branding, thought leadership, and direct recruitment. AI-driven algorithms personalize content feeds, job suggestions, and professional connections, making these platforms more relevant and valuable for job seekers.

Adapting to the Digital Job Search Landscape: Strategies for Success

To navigate this tech-driven job market effectively, job seekers must adopt a proactive approach to learning and adaptability. This includes staying abreast of emerging technologies, upskilling in digital competencies, and leveraging online platforms for networking and personal branding. Building a digital presence that reflects your professional identity and engaging with online communities related to your field can significantly enhance your visibility and attractiveness to potential employers.

In conclusion, the impact of emerging technologies on job searching is profound and multifaceted, offering both challenges and opportunities. As we venture further into this digital era, embracing these technologies and integrating them into your job search strategy is not just advantageous—it's imperative. They provide a competitive edge, enabling you to navigate the complexities of the modern job market with greater ease, efficiency, and insight. As you embark on this journey, let these technological advancements be your allies, guiding you toward a future where your career aspirations are not just envisioned but realized. Embrace this digital transformation with an open mind and a willingness to adapt, for it is in this confluence of technology and human aspiration that the future of job searching lies.

The Evolving Landscape of Remote and Flexible Work

In the ever-changing tapestry of the modern workplace, the rise of remote and flexible work arrangements stands as a testament to the transformative power of technology and changing societal norms. This shift towards a more adaptable work environment is not just a fleeting trend but a fundamental change that is reshaping the way we conceive of work, life balance, and career development. As we delve into this new paradigm, it's essential to understand the forces driving this change, the opportunities it presents, and the challenges it poses, ensuring that you, as a job seeker, are well-equipped to navigate this evolving landscape.

The Digital Revolution: A Catalyst for Change

The advent of high-speed internet, cloud computing, and collaborative software has dismantled the traditional boundaries of the office, enabling work to be done from virtually anywhere. This digital revolution has democratized access to opportunities, allowing individuals to work for global companies without the need to relocate, thus broadening the horizons for job seekers and employers alike.

The Shift in Work-Life Balance Priorities

Today's workforce, particularly among millennials and Gen Z, places a premium on work-life balance and flexibility. The ability to manage one's schedule, avoid long commutes, and work in an environment that suits one's personal and professional needs is increasingly seen not as a perk but as a fundamental aspect of job satisfaction and overall well-being.

The Response to Global Challenges

Recent global events, most notably the COVID-19 pandemic, have accelerated the adoption of remote work, proving its viability and efficiency across industries. This forced experiment has dispelled many myths surrounding remote work, highlighting its potential to maintain, if not enhance, productivity, creativity, and team cohesion.

The Opportunities: Access, Inclusion, and Sustainability

Remote and flexible work arrangements open doors to a more inclusive and diverse workforce, including those with disabilities, caregivers, and individuals in remote or underserved regions. Furthermore, the reduction in commuting contributes to environmental sustainability, aligning with growing ecological awareness and corporate responsibility initiatives.

The Challenges: Connectivity, Collaboration, and Culture

While the benefits are manifold, the shift to remote work also presents challenges. Ensuring reliable connectivity, fostering effective collaboration in a digital environment, and maintaining a cohesive company culture without physical interaction require innovative solutions and a proactive approach to communication and team dynamics.

Strategies for Job Seekers: Adapting to the New Normal

As a job seeker in this evolving landscape, it's crucial to develop skills that align with remote and flexible work. Proficiency in digital communication tools, self-discipline, time management, and the ability to work independently while being an effective team player are increasingly important. Building a personal brand that reflects your ability to thrive in a flexible work environment can set you apart.

The Future of Work: Hybrid Models and Beyond

Looking ahead, the future of work is likely to be characterized by hybrid models that blend remote and on-site work, offering flexibility while preserving the benefits of face-to-face interaction. Staying informed about trends and best practices in remote work, and continuously adapting your skills and work style, will be key to navigating this future successfully.

In conclusion, the evolving landscape of remote and flexible work represents a significant shift in the world of employment, offering new opportunities for career growth, work-life balance, and global collaboration. Embracing this change, honing the skills it demands, and staying adaptable in the face of its challenges will not only enhance your job search success but also position you to thrive in the careers of tomorrow. As we move forward, let this shift inspire us to reimagine the possibilities of work, fostering a more inclusive, sustainable, and fulfilling professional landscape.

Preparing for the Jobs of Tomorrow

As we stand at the threshold of a new era in the job market, the question isn't just about finding a job; it's about preparing for the jobs of tomorrow. The future of work is being sculpted by rapid technological advancements, shifts in global economic landscapes, and evolving societal values. In this dynamic environment, foresight, adaptability, and continuous learning are paramount. This chapter is dedicated to unraveling the complexities of this future, offering strategies and insights to ensure that you, as a job seeker, are not just ready but ahead of the curve, poised to seize the opportunities that tomorrow holds.

Anticipating the Future: Trends and Predictions

The future job market is anticipated to be marked by increased automation, the rise of artificial intelligence, and the proliferation of gig and remote work. These changes suggest a shift in the skills and competencies that employers will seek. Critical thinking, emotional intelligence, adaptability, and technological fluency are expected to be at a premium, alongside specialized skills in emerging fields such as renewable energy, AI, and biotechnology.

Lifelong Learning: The Non-negotiable Investment

In this ever-evolving landscape, the concept of lifelong learning has transitioned from a lofty ideal to a practical necessity. Staying abreast of industry trends, emerging technologies, and new methodologies is crucial. This commitment to learning can take many forms, from formal education and online courses to self-directed learning and on-the-job training. Embrace a learner's mindset, viewing each job, project, and experience as an opportunity to grow and expand your skillset.

Embracing Technological Proficiency

Technological proficiency is no longer confined to IT professionals. As digital tools permeate every aspect of work, a basic understanding of these technologies, their applications, and their implications for your field becomes essential. Whether it's mastering data analysis tools, understanding the basics of coding, or staying informed about AI and automation, technological literacy will be a key differentiator in the job market of tomorrow.

The Soft Skills Advantage

As machines take over more routine tasks, the human elements of work—creativity, empathy, communication, and leadership—will gain prominence. Cultivating these soft skills can enhance your ability to work effectively in teams, navigate complex social dynamics, and lead with vision and empathy. These skills, combined with technical expertise, will define the well-rounded professionals of the future.

Networking and Collaboration in a Digital Age

The ability to network and collaborate effectively, even in virtual environments, will continue to be a critical component of professional success. Building a diverse and global network, leveraging social media and professional platforms, and engaging in online communities can open doors to opportunities and insights that extend beyond geographical boundaries.

Adaptability and Resilience: The Core Competencies

In a world characterized by rapid change, adaptability and resilience emerge as core competencies. Cultivating a flexible mindset, being open to change, and developing strategies to manage stress and setbacks will equip you to navigate the uncertainties of the future job market with confidence and poise.

Preparing for Non-linear Career Paths

The linear career path is becoming a relic of the past. Be prepared for a career that might include multiple roles, industries, and even professions. This non-linear trajectory can be a source of strength, offering a broad perspective, a diverse skill set, and a rich tapestry of experiences.

In conclusion, preparing for the jobs of tomorrow is about more than just anticipating trends; it's about actively shaping your career trajectory with intention, curiosity, and resilience. As we explore the frontiers of the future job market, let's approach it with a spirit of adventure and a commitment to continuous growth. Armed with a diverse skill set, a global network, and a passion for lifelong learning, you are not just ready for the future; you are ready to lead it. Embrace this journey with an open heart and an eager mind, for in the landscape of tomorrow, every challenge is an opportunity, and every ending a new beginning.

Conclusion: Cultivating a Lifelong Career Strategy

Continuous Learning and Adaptation

In the realm of modern employment, where change is the only constant, embracing continuous learning and adaptation isn't just an advantage—it's a necessity. As we navigate through the chapters of our careers, we must recognize that the landscape is ever-evolving, driven by technological advancements, shifts in market demand, and the global economic climate. This dynamic environment requires us to be perpetual learners, always ready to acquire new skills and adapt to new challenges. This chapter is dedicated to instilling a mindset of growth and flexibility, ensuring that you remain not just relevant but ahead in the game of career development.

The Imperative of Lifelong Learning

Gone are the days when education ended at graduation. In today's fast-paced world, the pursuit of knowledge is unending. It's imperative to stay abreast of the latest trends, technologies, and methodologies in your field. This could mean pursuing formal education, such as advanced degrees or certifications, or engaging in self-directed learning through online courses, webinars, and workshops. Embracing a philosophy of lifelong learning demonstrates to potential employers your commitment to self-improvement and your capability to tackle the unknown.

Adapting to Technological Shifts

As digital transformation reshapes industries, understanding and leveraging the latest technologies become critical. Whether it's artificial intelligence, blockchain, or cloud computing, being proficient or at least familiar with these technologies can give you a significant edge. Engage with tech-focused communities, participate in hackathons, or simply experiment with new software and tools. Remember, in the digital age, technology is your ally.

Cultivating a Growth Mindset

At the heart of continuous learning is a growth mindset—the belief that your abilities and intelligence can be developed with effort, learning, and persistence. Challenges become opportunities to grow, and failures are merely stepping stones to success. Cultivating this mindset encourages resilience, a trait that is invaluable in the face of the inevitable setbacks and challenges that come with any career.

Building a Personal Learning Network

In the journey of lifelong learning, you're not alone. Building a network of mentors, peers, and thought leaders can provide support, inspiration, and a wealth of knowledge. Engage in professional associations, online forums, and social media groups relevant to your field. Sharing experiences and insights with others can accelerate your learning and open up new pathways for growth.

Adapting to Organizational and Role Changes

The concept of a career for life within a single organization is becoming increasingly rare. Be prepared to pivot, whether that means changing roles within your current organization, switching industries, or even starting your own venture. Adaptability is key—being open to change, willing to take risks, and capable of transferring your skills to new contexts.

Fostering Emotional Intelligence and Soft Skills

In an era where automation and AI are on the rise, the uniquely human skills of emotional intelligence, communication, and empathy become more critical than ever. Developing these soft skills can enhance your ability to work collaboratively, lead effectively, and navigate the complexities of workplace dynamics.

Embracing Change as the Only Constant

In conclusion, the path to career success in the modern era is not linear but a continuous cycle of learning, adapting, and growing. By embracing change, staying curious, and cultivating resilience, you position yourself to thrive amidst the uncertainties of the job market. Let this commitment to continuous learning and adaptation be your guiding principle, fueling your journey towards achieving mastery in your career. Remember, in the grand tapestry of your professional life, each learning experience, each adaptation, is a vibrant thread, weaving together a story of triumph and resilience.

Building and Maintaining Professional Relationships

In the intricate web of career development, professional relationships stand as the cornerstone, shaping paths, opening doors, and often determining the altitude of one's career trajectory. It is through these connections that opportunities are born, knowledge is shared, and support systems are built.

This chapter delves into the nuanced art of building and nurturing these vital connections, emphasizing the symbiotic nature of professional relationships and the impact they have on long-term career success.

The Foundation of Networking

Networking, at its core, is about establishing and fostering meaningful connections with individuals within and outside your industry. It goes beyond mere acquaintance to developing relationships that are mutually beneficial. The advent of digital platforms like LinkedIn has revolutionized networking, making it more accessible but also more nuanced. It's about engaging with your connections, understanding their needs, and offering value, whether it's through sharing insightful articles, participating in discussions, or introducing connections that might benefit from knowing each other.

Quality Over Quantity

In the pursuit of building a network, the emphasis must always be on the quality of connections rather than sheer numbers. It's about forging relationships that are profound and lasting. These are the connections that will vouch for you, offer you sage advice, and stand by you as you navigate the twists and turns of your career. It's about finding your tribe—a group of mentors, peers, and protégés with whom you can share, learn, and grow.

The Art of Follow-Up

The initial connection is just the beginning. The essence of networking lies in the follow-up. It's in the *'how have you been?'* messages, the coffee catch-ups, and the congratulatory notes on new milestones. It's about staying present and relevant in your connections' professional lives in a way that's genuine and heartfelt. Remember, a network thrives on reciprocity and regular nourishment.

Mentorship and Sponsorship

Within the realm of professional relationships, mentorship and sponsorship hold a special place. Mentors guide, advise, and support, helping you navigate the complexities of your career with their wisdom. Sponsors, on the other hand, are your champions in spaces where you're not present, advocating for your advancement. Cultivating these relationships requires not just respect and admiration but a genuine connection and understanding of mutual goals and values.

Embracing Diversity

A robust network is a diverse one. It spans different industries, roles, cultures, and perspectives. Diversity in your professional network exposes you to different viewpoints, challenges your assumptions, and enriches your understanding of the world. It makes you more adaptable, innovative, and inclusive—a vital trait in today's global job market.

Navigating the Digital and Physical Networking Worlds

While online networking platforms offer convenience and reach, the importance of face-to-face interactions remains undiminished. Conferences, workshops, and industry meet-ups provide opportunities for more personal interactions, allowing for a different level of connection. Balancing digital and in-person networking efforts is key, leveraging the strengths of each to build a comprehensive and effective network.

In Conclusion: The Lifeline of Your Career

As we wrap up this exploration into building and maintaining professional relationships, remember that these connections are not just a means to an end. They are the lifeline of your career, offering support, inspiration, and opportunities. Treat them with care, invest time and energy into them, and watch as they grow and flourish alongside your career. Remember, in the grand narrative of your professional journey, the relationships you cultivate and nurture are the chapters that add depth, color, and vibrancy, transforming your career into a rich tapestry of interconnected experiences and shared successes.

The Path Forward: Embracing Change and Opportunity

As we stand at the threshold of the future, the path forward in the realm of job hunting and career development is both exhilarating and daunting. The landscape of employment is continuously evolving, shaped by technological advancements, shifts in the global economy, and changing societal norms. The key to navigating this ever-changing terrain lies in embracing change and recognizing the plethora of opportunities it brings.

Adapting to Technological Disruptions

The digital age has transformed the way we seek and secure employment. From AI-powered job matching platforms to virtual reality job simulations, technology has opened new frontiers in job hunting.

It's imperative to stay abreast of these advancements, not just as tools for finding opportunities but as skills and knowledge areas to enhance employability. Continuous learning and upskilling have become more than just advice; they are necessities in remaining relevant in a job market that prizes digital literacy and technological proficiency.

The Gig Economy and Beyond

The rise of the gig economy has redefined traditional career paths, offering flexibility and autonomy but also demanding a higher level of self-motivation and adaptability. Navigating this gig landscape requires a shift in mindset—from viewing employment as a linear path to seeing it as a mosaic of diverse, often concurrent, professional experiences. It's about leveraging each gig not just for income but as stepping stones for skill development, networking, and personal branding.

Global Opportunities and Challenges

In an increasingly interconnected world, job seekers are no longer confined to local opportunities. Remote work, digital nomadism, and international collaborations have expanded horizons, making it essential to develop cross-cultural competencies and global awareness. However, this global playground also brings challenges, from navigating international job markets and work visas to understanding diverse workplace cultures. The ability to adapt, communicate, and work effectively across cultures is becoming a pivotal skill.

Personal Branding in a Digital World

In the digital era, personal branding has taken on a new dimension. It's not just about how you present yourself in interviews or networking events but how you're perceived online. A carefully curated digital presence that showcases your professional achievements, thought leadership, and personality can set you apart. It's about creating a cohesive narrative that reflects your professional identity, values, and aspirations.

Emotional Intelligence and Resilience

As automation and AI take over routine tasks, the human qualities of empathy, creativity, and resilience become more valuable. Emotional intelligence—the ability to be aware of, control, and express one's emotions, and to handle interpersonal relationships judiciously and empathetically—is emerging as a critical skill. Similarly, resilience—the capacity to recover quickly from difficulties—is essential in a landscape where change is the only constant.

Collaboration and Co-creation

The future of work is collaborative. The ability to work effectively in teams, to co-create with colleagues across different functions, and to drive innovation through collective effort is paramount. It's about moving beyond competition to collaboration, recognizing that the most groundbreaking solutions often come from diverse minds working together.

Conclusion: A Journey of Continuous Evolution

As we conclude this exploration of the path forward, it's clear that the future of job hunting and career development is not just about navigating change but about embracing it as an opportunity for growth, learning, and exploration. It's about viewing your career not as a ladder to be climbed but as a landscape to be navigated, with each experience enriching your professional journey. Remember, in this ever-evolving world, your ability to adapt, learn, and innovate is your most valuable asset. So, embrace the journey with openness, curiosity, and resilience, and let the adventure unfold.

Appendices

Recommended Resources and Tools

In the labyrinth of job hunting, having the right tools and resources can illuminate your path, guiding you towards your career goals with precision and efficiency. As your companion in this journey, I've curated a list of indispensable resources and tools that have not only stood the test of time but have also adapted to the evolving job market dynamics. These resources span across various stages of job searching, from discovery to application, networking, and beyond.

Job Boards and Aggregators

- **LinkedIn**: Beyond a networking platform, LinkedIn serves as a vital job board where opportunities across industries are posted daily. Its job search functionality allows for customized searches based on industry, role, location, and experience level.

- **Indeed**: A powerhouse in job aggregation, Indeed compiles listings from thousands of websites, including job boards, staffing firms, and company career pages, offering a comprehensive view of the market.

- **Glassdoor**: While known for company reviews, Glassdoor also offers a robust job search engine and insights into company cultures, salary benchmarks, and interview processes.

Niche Industry Websites

- **AngelList**: For those in the startup ecosystem, AngelList is the go-to platform for opportunities in emerging companies.

- **Behance**: Creative professionals can showcase their portfolios and discover job opportunities in design, photography, and other creative fields.

- **Stack Overflow**: A haven for developers and programmers, Stack Overflow offers job listings alongside its well-known developer community and Q&A section.

Networking and Personal Branding

- **Meetup**: This platform allows you to find and join groups related to professional interests and industries, facilitating in-person or virtual networking events.

- **Canva**: A user-friendly graphic design tool that can help in creating professional-looking personal branding materials, including resumes, business cards, and portfolio presentations.

Resume Builders and Career Tools

- **Zety**: This online resume builder offers customizable templates, making it easier to create professional resumes tailored to specific job applications.

- **Jobscan**: A tool designed to optimize resumes and cover letters for applicant tracking systems (ATS), ensuring higher visibility in automated screenings.

Learning and Skill Development

- **Coursera** and **edX**: Both platforms offer courses from universities and colleges around the world, covering a vast range of subjects including business, technology, and personal development.

- **Udemy**: With a focus on professional and personal growth, Udemy provides courses on everything from software development to public speaking.

Interview Preparation

- **Big Interview**: An online system that combines training and practice to help improve your interview technique and build confidence.

- **LeetCode**: For those in tech, practicing coding problems on LeetCode can be a crucial step in preparing for technical interviews.

Freelancing and Gig Work

- **Upwork** and **Fiverr**: These platforms offer freelancers the opportunity to find short-term work or gigs in their area of expertise, from writing and graphic design to web development and digital marketing.

Conclusion: A Toolkit for Success

Equipping yourself with these resources and tools is akin to arming yourself for a journey. Each one has the potential to open new doors, illuminate hidden opportunities, and pave the way for successful career advancements. Remember, the landscape of employment is ever-changing, and so should your toolkit. Stay adaptable, keep exploring new resources, and never cease to enrich your arsenal. With the right tools in hand, the path forward is not just about embracing change and opportunity; it's about creating it.

Glossary of Key Terms

In the realm of job hunting and career development, terminology can often become a maze of jargon and buzzwords that may seem daunting at first glance. In this section, I aim to demystify some of these terms, providing clear and concise definitions to enhance your understanding and empower your job search journey.

- **Applicant Tracking System (ATS)**: A software application that enables the electronic handling of recruitment needs. An ATS can be used to post job openings on a corporate website or job board, screen resumes, and generate interview requests to potential candidates by email.
- **Branding (Personal Branding)**: The practice of marketing yourself and your career as brands. Personal branding is the conscious and intentional effort to create and influence public perception by positioning oneself as an authority in their industry, elevating their

credibility, and differentiating themselves from the competition.

- **Career Transition**: The process of changing one's occupation or career path. This could involve moving to a new industry, starting a new role that utilizes different skills, or a complete overhaul of one's professional direction.

- **Cover Letter**: A written document submitted with a job application explaining the applicant's credentials and interest in the open position. Unlike a resume, a cover letter allows you to introduce yourself in a more personal manner, highlighting key achievements and explaining why you're the best fit for the role.

- **Employment Ecosystem**: Refers to the interconnected and dynamic network of employers, employees, regulatory institutions, educational entities, and job market trends that collectively influence the employment landscape.

- **Freelancing**: The act of working as an independent contractor rather than being employed by someone else. Freelancers are self-employed and often referred to as independent contractors, free agents, or gig workers.

- **Gig Economy**: A labor market characterized by the prevalence of short-term contracts or freelance work as opposed to permanent jobs. Individuals work gigs, which are temporary, flexible jobs that companies or people hire independent contractors for.

- **Informational Interview**: An interview conducted to gather information about a job, career field, industry, or company culture. This is not a job interview, but rather an opportunity for job seekers to learn more and network with professionals in their desired field.

- **LinkedIn Optimization**: The process of enhancing one's LinkedIn profile for better visibility and networking opportunities. This involves using strategic keywords, highlighting achievements, and engaging with content to improve one's presence on the platform.

- **Networking**: The act of interacting with others to exchange information and develop professional or social contacts. Effective networking involves building and maintaining relationships that could lead to job opportunities, career advancement, and professional growth.

- **Quantifying Achievements**: The practice of adding measurable metrics to your accomplishments. Instead of stating responsibilities, you illustrate your achievements with numbers, percentages, or other concrete data to provide a clear picture of your impact.

- **Remote Work**: A working style that allows professionals to work outside of a traditional office environment. It is based on the concept that work does not need to be done in a specific place to be executed successfully.

- **Resume**: A document that presents a person's background, skills, and accomplishments. Resumes are most commonly used to secure new employment, often accompanied by a customized cover letter.

- **Skill Gap**: The difference between skills that employers need to achieve their goals and the skills that their employees have. Identifying and addressing skill gaps is crucial for career advancement and job market relevance.

- **Transferable Skills**: Skills that are valuable in many different jobs and industries. They can be transferred from one job to another, making them particularly important during career transitions.

As you navigate through your job hunt and career development, understanding these key terms will not only enhance your communication but also deepen your insights into the employment world. By familiarizing yourself with this vocabulary, you're equipping yourself with the knowledge to make informed decisions and take strategic actions toward your career triumph.

Checklist for Job Hunters

Embarking on a job hunt can often feel like setting sail in uncharted waters. To navigate these waters with confidence, it's imperative to have a compass and a map; in the realm of job hunting, this translates to a comprehensive checklist. This checklist is designed to be your steadfast companion, guiding you through each phase of your job search with precision and clarity.

Preparation Phase:
- **Self-Assessment**: Reflect on your skills, interests, and values. Use tools like SWOT analysis to understand your strengths, weaknesses, opportunities, and threats.

- **Career Goals**: Define clear, measurable, and achievable career objectives. Consider both short-term and long-term aspirations.

- **Skill Enhancement**: Identify any skill gaps and seek out resources for learning, such as online courses on platforms like Coursera, Udemy, or LinkedIn Learning.

- **Resume Building**: Craft a compelling resume that highlights your achievements and skills. Tailor it for each application to align with the job description.

- **Cover Letter Crafting**: Develop a customizable cover letter template that you can adapt for different job applications, making sure to address the specific requirements and values of each employer.

Job Search Phase:

- **Job Boards and Websites**: Regularly visit job boards like Indeed, Glassdoor, and niche industry-specific sites. Set up alerts for your desired job titles and companies.

- **LinkedIn Optimization**: Update your LinkedIn profile with a professional photo, compelling summary, and detailed experience. Use keywords strategically to increase visibility.

- **Networking**: Engage in both online and offline networking. Join professional groups, attend industry meetups, and participate in webinars and forums in your field.

- **Informational Interviews**: Reach out to professionals in your desired field for informational interviews. Prepare thoughtful questions to gain insights into the industry and potential job opportunities.

Application Phase:

- **Customized Applications**: Tailor each application to the job and company. Highlight relevant experience and how you can add value to the specific role.

- **ATS Optimization**: Use keywords from the job description in your resume and cover letter to ensure they pass through Applicant Tracking Systems.

- **Follow-Up**: After submitting an application, follow up with a polite email to reiterate your interest and inquire about the status of your application.

Interview Preparation Phase:

- **Research**: Thoroughly research the company, its culture, recent achievements, and the interviewers, if known.

- **Mock Interviews**: Practice answering common interview questions and conduct mock interviews with friends or through professional services.

- **Questions for Employers**: Prepare insightful questions to ask your interviewers, demonstrating your interest in the role and the company.

Post-Interview Phase:

- **Thank-You Note**: Send a personalized thank-you email to each interviewer within 24 hours, summarizing your enthusiasm for the role and key points discussed.

- **Offer Evaluation**: When you receive a job offer, carefully evaluate the terms, benefits, and alignment with your career goals. Consider the company culture and growth opportunities.

Continuous Learning and Networking:

- **Professional Development**: Stay committed to continuous learning and skill development, even after securing a job. This ensures you remain competitive and adaptable in your career.

- **Maintain Relationships**: Keep in touch with your professional network, offering help and sharing knowledge. Remember, networking is a two-way street.

This checklist is not merely a set of tasks but a blueprint for strategic, informed, and focused job hunting. By adhering to this guide, you position yourself not just as a job seeker, but as a discerning professional poised for career triumph. As you journey through these steps, remember that each application, each interview, and each networking opportunity is a step closer to your career aspirations. With diligence, resilience, and the right strategies, the path forward is yours to carve.

Summary

Introduction: The Art of the Job Hunt in the Modern Era 3
    Embracing the New Job Market Landscape 3
    The Philosophy Behind Effective Job Searching 6
        Understanding Yourself: The Keystone of Job Searching 6
        Adapting to Change: The Only Constant in the Job Market 6
        The Power of Networking: Building Bridges, Not Just Contacts 7
        Leveraging Technology: The Double-Edged Sword 7
        Resilience: The Art of Bouncing Back 8
        A Lifelong Pursuit: Career Development as a Continuous Journey 8

Chapter 1: Laying the Groundwork for Success 10
    Self-Assessment: Identifying Your Unique Skills and Interests 10
        The Mirror of Self-Reflection 10
        Decoding Skills and Strengths 11
        The Inventory of Achievements 11
        The Landscape of Interests 11
        The Alignment of Values 12
        The Power of Feedback 12
        Crafting Your Professional Narrative 12
    Understanding the Employment Ecosystem 13
        The Industry Terrain: A Tapestry of Opportunities 14

- The Job Market Climate: Navigating Trends and Shifts 14
  - Technological Currents: The Winds of Change 15
  - The Networking Web: Fostering Connections and Synergies 15
    - Skill Evolution: Adapting to the Habitat 16
    - Cultural Diversity: The Ecosystem's Rich Biodiversity 16
  - Setting Realistic and Ambitious Career Goals 18
    - Breaking Down the Vision: Milestones and Steps 18
    - Market Alignment: Ensuring Your Goals Are In Sync With Reality 19
    - Flexibility: The Ability to Pivot 19
    - Action Plan: Mapping the Journey 20
    - Accountability and Review: Keeping on Track 20
    - Integrating Personal and Professional Goals: A Holistic Approach 21
- Chapter 2: The Digital Toolbox: Online Resources and Platforms 22
  - Navigating Job Boards and Career Websites 22
    - Understanding the Terrain: Job Boards and Career Websites 22
    - Creating a Strategic Approach: Quality Over Quantity 23
    - Leveraging Advanced Search Features: The Key to Precision 23
    - Researching Employers: Going Beyond the Job Posting 24

Networking and Engagement: The Human Element ..24

Tracking and Organization: Navigating with Precision 25

Continuous Learning and Adaptation: Evolving with the Landscape 25

Leveraging LinkedIn: Beyond the Basics 26

Crafting a Compelling Profile: Your Digital Handshake 27

Showcasing Your Experience: More Than a Job Title .27

Skills and Endorsements: A Testament to Your Abilities 28

Recommendations: The Power of Professional Testimonials 28

Engaging with Content: Demonstrating Thought Leadership 28

Networking Strategically: Building Meaningful Connections 29

Utilizing LinkedIn Jobs and Alerts: Staying Ahead of Opportunities 29

Utilizing Niche Industry Websites for Targeted Searches 31

The Essence of Niche Job Boards: A Specialized Approach 31

Identifying Relevant Niche Sites: The First Step to Targeted Search 32

Creating a Standout Presence: Beyond the Basic Profile 32

Leveraging Insights and Resources: More Than Job Listings 33

Networking Within Niche Communities: Building Meaningful Connections 33

Applying with Precision: Tailored Applications for Targeted Roles 33

Staying Informed and Adaptable: Keeping Up with Industry Evolution 34

Chapter 3: The Power of Networking: Strategies and Etiquette 36

Crafting Your Personal Brand 36

Defining Your Core: The Foundation of Your Brand ... 36

Articulating Your Value Proposition: Your Professional Promise 37

Consistency Across Platforms: Unified and Cohesive 37

Visibility and Thought Leadership: Sharing Your Insights 38

Networking with Authenticity: Building Professional Relationships 38

Feedback and Evolution: A Dynamic Process 39

Living Your Brand: Beyond Online Presence 39

Effective Networking: Online and Offline Tactics 40

Online Networking: Harnessing the Power of Digital Platforms 40

Offline Networking: The Irreplaceable Value of Personal Interaction 42

Blending Online and Offline Tactics: A Synergistic Approach 43

Networking Etiquette: The Art of Authentic Engagement 43

Follow-Up: Cultivating and Maintaining Connections 44

Informational Interviews: How to Approach and Benefit from Them...45

The Essence of Informational Interviews: A Strategic Exploration...45

Identifying Potential Interviewees: Casting a Wide Net 46

Crafting Your Approach: The Art of the Ask..................46

Preparation is Key: Doing Your Homework 46

Navigating the Conversation: Active Listening and Engagement 47

The Follow-Up: Cultivating a Lasting Connection 47

Leveraging Insights: Applying What You Learn 48

Chapter 4: Crafting Winning Resumes and Cover Letters...49

The Art of Personalizing Your Application 49

Understanding the Role and Company: The Foundation of Personalization..49

Customizing Your Resume: A Reflection of Fit and Value 50

The Cover Letter: Your Narrative Bridge.......................50

Leveraging LinkedIn and Social Media: Consistent Personal Branding...51

Engagement and Follow-Up: Demonstrating Interest and Initiative..51

Seeking Feedback for Continuous Improvement..........52

Keywords and SEO: Optimizing for Applicant Tracking Systems..53

Deciphering the Algorithm: Understanding ATS Mechanics 53

Strategic Keyword Integration: Speaking the ATS Language.. 54

Beyond Keywords: The Nuance of SEO in Job Applications 54

Formatting for Clarity: Making it ATS-Friendly............ 55

Customization is Key: Tailoring for Each Application 55

Leveraging LinkedIn and Online Profiles for SEO 55

Continuous Learning and Adaptation: Staying Ahead of the Curve... 56

Showcasing Achievements: Quantifying Success.............. 57

The Power of Quantification: Making Success Measurable 57

Identifying Quantifiable Achievements: A Strategic Review 58

Crafting Achievement Statements: The Art of Precision and Relevance... 58

Contextualizing Achievements: Beyond Numbers 59

Incorporating Achievements Across Your Application Materials 59

Tailoring Achievements to Each Application: The Custom Fit... 60

The Continuous Evolution of Your Achievement Portfolio 60

Chapter 5: Acing the Interview and Beyond............................ 62

Preparing for Different Types of Interviews 62

Traditional Interviews: The Art of Conversational Mastery... 62

Behavioral Interviews: Storytelling with Purpose....... 63

Group Interviews: Navigating the Dynamics of Collective Evaluation 63

Panel Interviews: Managing Multiple Evaluators 64

Virtual Interviews: Mastering the Digital Domain 64

Stress Interviews: Keeping Composure Under Pressure 65

Preparation Beyond the Interview Type: The Holistic Approach 65

Communicating Your Value: Strategies for Success 66

Understanding Your Unique Selling Proposition (USP) 67

Crafting a Compelling Narrative 67

Elevating Your Resume and LinkedIn Profile 68

Mastering the Elevator Pitch 68

Interview Strategies: Demonstrating Value in Real-Time 69

Negotiating Offers: Articulating Your Worth 69

Continuous Self-Development and Reassessment 69

Negotiating Offers and Evaluating Opportunities 70

Understanding Your Worth: The Bedrock of Negotiation 71

Comprehensive Evaluation: Beyond the Paycheck 71

Effective Negotiation Tactics: Balancing Assertiveness with Diplomacy 72

Leveraging Multiple Offers: A Strategic Advantage 72

The Art of Declining Gracefully: Maintaining Professional Relationships 73

Seeking Clarity and Confirmation: Ensuring Mutual Understanding 73

Reflection and Forward-Thinking: The Path Ahead.... 73

Chapter 6: Navigating Job Market Challenges 75

Overcoming Common Obstacles in Job Searching 75

Facing Rejection: Building Resilience and Insight 75

Navigating the ATS Maze: Mastering the Digital Gatekeeper 76

Bridging Employment Gaps: Crafting a Positive Narrative 76

Overcoming Overqualification Concerns: Balancing Expertise and Flexibility 77

Expanding a Limited Network: Strategic Connection Building 77

Staying Current in a Rapidly Evolving Job Market: Continuous Learning 78

Maintaining Motivation: Setting Realistic Goals and Celebrating Progress 78

Embracing Career Transitions and Change 79

Understanding the Nature of Career Transitions 80

Self-Assessment: Realigning Your Compass 80

Skill Bridging: Building the Foundation for New Beginnings 81

Networking: Navigating the New Terrain with Allies 81

Personal Branding: Redefining Your Professional Identity 82

Embracing a Growth Mindset: The Learner's Journey 82

Practical Steps: From Planning to Action 82

Staying Motivated and Resilient 83

    Cultivating a Growth Mindset: The Foundation of Resilience 84

    Setting Realistic, Achievable Goals: Navigating with Purpose 85

    Maintaining a Balanced Perspective: Beyond the Job Search 85

    Leveraging Your Support System: Strength in Community 86

    Embracing Self-Care: The Reservoir of Strength 86

    Adopting a Long-Term Vision: Navigating the Bigger Picture 86

Chapter 7: The Future of Job Hunting: Trends and Predictions 88

    Emerging Technologies and Their Impact on Job Searching 88

    Artificial Intelligence and Machine Learning: Personalizing the Job Search 88

    Big Data: Insights and Opportunities................................89

    Virtual Reality: The Future of Recruitment and Onboarding..89

    Blockchain: Credential Verification and Trust...............90

    Social Media and Networking Platforms: Expanding Horizons 90

    Adapting to the Digital Job Search Landscape: Strategies for Success 91

The Evolving Landscape of Remote and Flexible Work ..92

    The Digital Revolution: A Catalyst for Change 93

- The Shift in Work-Life Balance Priorities 93
- The Response to Global Challenges 93
- The Opportunities: Access, Inclusion, and Sustainability 94
- The Challenges: Connectivity, Collaboration, and Culture 94
- Strategies for Job Seekers: Adapting to the New Normal 95
- The Future of Work: Hybrid Models and Beyond 95
- Preparing for the Jobs of Tomorrow 96
  - Anticipating the Future: Trends and Predictions 96
  - Lifelong Learning: The Non-negotiable Investment ... 97
  - Embracing Technological Proficiency 97
  - The Soft Skills Advantage 98
  - Networking and Collaboration in a Digital Age 98
  - Adaptability and Resilience: The Core Competencies 98
  - Preparing for Non-linear Career Paths 99
- Conclusion: Cultivating a Lifelong Career Strategy 100
  - Continuous Learning and Adaptation 100
    - The Imperative of Lifelong Learning 100
    - Adapting to Technological Shifts 101
    - Cultivating a Growth Mindset 101
    - Building a Personal Learning Network 102
    - Adapting to Organizational and Role Changes 102
    - Fostering Emotional Intelligence and Soft Skills 102
    - Embracing Change as the Only Constant 103

- Building and Maintaining Professional Relationships .. 103
  - The Foundation of Networking 104
  - Quality Over Quantity 104
  - The Art of Follow-Up 105
  - Mentorship and Sponsorship 105
  - Embracing Diversity 106
  - Navigating the Digital and Physical Networking Worlds 106
  - In Conclusion: The Lifeline of Your Career 106
- The Path Forward: Embracing Change and Opportunity 107
  - Adapting to Technological Disruptions 107
  - The Gig Economy and Beyond 108
  - Global Opportunities and Challenges 108
  - Personal Branding in a Digital World 109
  - Emotional Intelligence and Resilience 109
  - Collaboration and Co-creation 110
  - Conclusion: A Journey of Continuous Evolution 110
- Appendices 111
  - Recommended Resources and Tools 111
    - Job Boards and Aggregators 111
    - Niche Industry Websites 112
    - Networking and Personal Branding 112
    - Resume Builders and Career Tools 113
    - Learning and Skill Development 113
    - Interview Preparation 114

    Freelancing and Gig Work 114
    Conclusion: A Toolkit for Success 114
Glossary of Key Terms 115
Checklist for Job Hunters 119

www.ingramcontent.com/pod-product-compliance
Lightning Source LLC
Chambersburg PA
CBHW050303230526
45471CB00005B/2004